The Destiny of Isabelle Eberhardt

The Destiny of

Isabelle Eberhardt

CECILY MACKWORTH

THE ECCO PRESS   NEW YORK

First published by The Ecco Press in 1975
Paperback edition published in 1986
18 West 30th Street, New York, N.Y. 10001

Library of Congress Cataloging in Publication Data
Mackworth, Cecily.
The destiny of Isabelle Eberhardt.

1. Eberhardt, Isabelle, 1877-1904.   I. Title.
DT294.-7.E2M3 1975   965 .03 0924 [B]   75-12764
ISBN 0-912-94622-9

PRINTED IN THE UNITED STATES OF AMERICA
The Ecco Press logo by Ahmed Yacoubi

Illustrations

Preface

I should like to thank all those people—in Paris, in Geneva, in Algiers—who have made it possible for me to trace the life and reconstitute the personality of Isabelle Eberhardt. First of all I should mention René-Louis Doyon who discovered and published her diaries, some important letters and a number of short stories and who has allowed me to quote freely from all of these; and Madame Barrucand who, in Algiers, put at my disposition all the unpublished correspondence in the possession of the late M. Victor Barrucand and allowed me to examine the manuscripts retrieved from the flood at Ain-Sefra.

Acknowledgements are also due to Monsieur Robert Randau who has permitted me to reproduce a long letter written to him by the Foreign Legionary, Richard Kohn and numerous details on Isabelle's life in Tenes; to M. Raoul Stéphan; to Colonel Delabaye for information on Isabelle's activities in southern Oran at the time of the penetration of Morocco; to M. Octave Depont for details on the Islamic confraternities; to Professor Weber, of the Faculty of Medicine in Geneva, who helped me to discover at least something of the truth about Isabelle's early life in Switzerland.

I should also like to thank a number of elderly people who have given me the benefit of their personal reminiscences: Mademoiselle Marie Perez-Moreyra in Geneva, Commandant Cauvet and Madame Randau in Algiers, the Bachagha Masraeli-abdul-Aziz in El Oued.

Chapter One

ARLY in the eighteen-sixties a certain General Paul de Moerder, a Russian of noble birth and officer in Tsar Alexander's Imperial Army, married a young girl of charming appearance, named Nathalie Eberhardt. She was tall, fair, slender and her whole manner was graceful and gentle. She was known to be a foreigner, a German of the Lutheran religion, and the General was probably too madly in love to inquire closely into her origin. At some time or another he must have discovered that she was the illegitimate child of a certain Fraulein Eberhardt and of a wealthy Russian Jew named Nicolas Korff, who had refused or been unable to give his daughter his own name. From that time on the poor man's life must have been a continual terror of discovery, since only those of unimpeachable birth could aspire to serve the Tsar in such a high capacity and the alliances of his officers were as strictly scrutinized as their own origins.

Perhaps this secret was the real explanation of the General's terrible character, for he was hated by his equals and dreaded by his subordinates. Although his passion for his wife never diminished, he must have resented bitterly the shame she had brought on him and, perhaps, the trick she had played on him, for it is unlikely that he was in full possession of the facts before his marriage. It was unfortunate enough to have married a bourgeoise, but the fact she was illegitimate and a demi-Jewess must have made his situation untenable. Anti-Semitism was so rife in the rigid and aristocratic Tsarist Army at that period that Jews were often known to commit suicide rather than undergo the horrors of their military service. If his fellow officers had suspected Paul de Moerder's lapse, his existence would have become unsupportable.

A number of children were born to this tormented couple —Nicolas in 1864, Nathalie in 1865 and Vladimir in 1868. The General, anxious to give them the best education possible, decided to engage a tutor, and, when Nicolas was of an age to learn to read, a pope of the Russian Orthodox Church, named Alexander Trophimovsky, was introduced into the household.

Trophimovsky was a remarkable man, both by his physique and his attainments. He was of Armenian origin and, although he was already in the late forties, he had the perfectly cut, classic profile, the soft dark eyes and the harmonious frame that is often found among the men of that race. He was also a scholar who had studied philosophy, knew Latin and Greek, spoke Turkish, Arabic and German as well as Russian. His manner was reserved and courteous and he quickly established his authority over the turbulent children. General de Moerder could congratulate himself on his choice, although he probably took little interest in the intellectual qualifications of his employee. Madame de Moerder, on the other hand, found in his conversation a distraction from her husband's well-meaning brutality and primitive mentality. The pope soon confided in her that he had long ago rejected Christianity and adopted the nihilist doctrine that was gaining more and more adherents among the Russian intellectuals. The events of 1848 had produced a belated effect even in this most autocratic and reactionary of societies. The tyranny of the Tsar, the serfdom of the masses, the attitude of the Army and the Church that blindly supported an authority that took no heed of justice, had exhausted the patience of a people accustomed to resignation and obedience. The doctrines of Socialism, which generally comprised at this period the components of political anarchism and philosophical nihilism, were sweeping through the universities in spite of wholesale deportations to Siberia. There were secret meetings, plots, sometimes assassinations, for the anarchists were convinced of the necessity for terrorism. Above all they sought to destroy the 'conventional lies of civilization', basis of an unjust society. Religion was for them the arch-lie and conventional morality an excuse for maintaining the inexcusable old order.

Trophimovsky had known Bakunin and been influenced by Tolstoy, although a certain element of caution in his character had restrained him from taking any active part in their campaigns. He may have been thrown out of the Church or he may have left it of his own will. His extreme bitterness against Christianity inclined people to believe the first explanation. His personality was extremely powerful and he had little difficulty in making a convert of the gentle, rather foolish woman who had plenty of leisure in which to listen to his tirades. His physical charm did the rest. One day the General returned to find his home deserted. His wife had disappeared with the interesting tutor, taking with her his three children. Trophimovsky, for his part, had left a wife and four children behind him in his native Kherson.

The couple fled first to Turkey, where Trophimovsky probably had relations. They remained for a time in Istanbul, then moved to Naples. Both were vague, rootless people, unable to settle or to adapt themselves to their situation. Madame de Moerder, accustomed to a solid and enviable position as the wife of an aristocrat and high-ranking officer, found herself an outlaw. There must have been slights from high-ranking Italian families, for the irascible lover would hardly have consented to remain in the shade. Money was scarce too; there were difficulties and disappointments and Trophimovsky, whose action does not seem to have been entirely disinterested, became more and more embittered. Since nothing bound them to Naples more than to any other city, they moved again and roamed around Italy, driven on by Trophimovsky's eternal dissatisfaction. Sometimes Madame de Moerder was accompanied by all her children, sometimes by one or other of them. Then, still unsettled and still avid for novelty, they came to Switzerland, where so many of their compatriots lived in exile, starved and plotted against the hated Alexander II.

Meanwhile, the General had never reconciled himself to the loss of his wife, whom he loved desperately in spite of all the trouble she had caused him. He had kept track of the truants, perhaps remained in correspondence with them, and now arrived in Switzerland to attempt a reconciliation. He must have succeeded for a time, since Trophimovsky came to Geneva, while Madame de Moerder stayed first in Zürich, then in Montreux, where a fourth child was born in 1872. He was named Augustin and recognized by the General, so perhaps he was an authentic de Moerder, although his presumed father returned to Russia about the time of his birth.

A year later the General died, leaving his fortune, which was considerable, to his wife but stipulating that the capital should remain blocked in Russia and that the revenues could only be paid abroad on condition that they were personally applied for at regular intervals.

During the next five years, the widow, the ex-tutor and the four children continued to lead an aimless and errant existence, alleviated by the comfortable income from the de Moerder estates. Madame de Moerder herself made one or two journeys to Russia on business, but she soon found it more convenient to give a procuration to Trophimovsky and allow him to settle her affairs. It was thus that her fortune began to drift gradually into the hands of her lover.

It was during one of these absences of Trophimovsky that Madame de Moerder gave birth on 17th February 1877 to a daughter in a maternity clinic in Geneva. The child was registered in the name of Isabelle Wilhelmine Marie and given the surname of Eberhardt in which her mother had contracted her marriage. Trophimovsky never recognized her as his daughter, perhaps on account of the nihilist principles which considered the family as one of the mainstays of an evil society, but he accepted her presence with joy, partly for love of her mother and partly because he considered a newborn baby as excellent raw material on which to try out some curious educational theories.

The family had grown so cumbersome by now that its former nomadic existence was no longer possible. Trophimovsky was ageing, Madame de Moerder no longer young. It was time to settle down. Soon after Isabelle's birth, Trophimovsky bought—in his own name but no doubt with Madame de Moerder's money—a house in the commune of Vernier on the outskirts of Geneva.

The Villa Neuve stood on the Route de Meyrin, which was in those days a lonely road leading off the highway in the direction of Lyons. A wooded common stretched on either side and neighbours were few. The Villa itself was a spacious house, standing in huge, rambling grounds, walled in, shaded by ancient trees and vaguely sad and sinister. The former inhabitants had introduced a number of tropical plants which flourished in the large conservatories adjoining the building, and Trophimovsky, something of a botanist, was fired at once with a passion for horticulture. He decided to raise cactus, built a rock garden and introduced rare shrubs, but failed to give them proper attention. When the plants drooped, he aspired to rear trout in a sort of moat that bordered the garden, and set to work, while the villagers, who were suspicious of the eccentric household, watched the experiment with stolid hostility. The trout died and were replaced by ducks. Then the ducks disappeared and the ex-pope hurled accusations of theft. His milk was laced with water too and he accused the tradesmen of cheating him. Indeed, he was a suspicious man, ready to believe the worst of everyone and irritable in spite of his professed fatalism.

Everything about the household aroused the distrust of the rare neighbours . . . the irregular situation of its inhabitants;

their unmistakably foreign appearance and accents; the curious manners of the master of the house who, when occasional visitors were present, was apt to yell out, apropos of nothing, 'Jesus Christ was a villain!' while pounding a powerful fist on the table; the sight of the pale, drooping boys who appeared to have no occupation and no interests and who received no regular education.

Trophimovsky in fact was growing more and more bitter and disillusioned. He avoided his compatriots, for, although he professed anarchist doctrines, the enthusiasm of the over-exalted men and women who had come into exile for their faith, tired and angered him. He had no faith in human nature or its perfectibility and preferred to retire into an ever stricter seclusion and occupy himself with endless projects for the house and garden, all of which regularly came to nothing.

The villa itself bore witness to the irresolute spirit and lack of concentration of its inhabitants. Everything about it seemed incomplete. The furniture was insufficient, so that it gave an impression of discomfort. Trophimovsky, who counted painting among his many talents, had started to stencil a fresco around the drawing-room walls, but had lost interest half-way round. The only really homely and pleasant thing in the house was the samovar around which the whole family assembled for constant tea-drinking. Then Madame de Moerder could imagine herself back in Russia, secure, respected and surrounded by elegant officers and beautiful women bearing great names. She suffered constantly from the segregation imposed on her by her illegal liaison and could not resign herself to the loss of her social position. Perhaps she had deeper causes for grief, for her daughter spoke later of the terrible wrongs suffered by her. Whatever these wrongs were, she recounted them endlessly to her children, inspiring them with a passionate longing to avenge her and an equally passionate hatred of the society from which she had suffered. The letters and papers which might have revealed the truth have been destroyed long ago. Isabelle's later diary contains only dark hints, an obsession and a desire for vengeance which her mother's death only served to inflame.

These children had a singular upbringing. None of them went to school, for Trophimovsky considered State education as one of the roots of the misfortunes of the human race, but he taught them himself, and they were more learned as a result than any normal schooling could have made them. At an early age they knew Greek and Latin and had at least a smattering of classical Arabic; they spoke French, German, Italian and Russian; they studied philosophy and read a vast number of books without any orderly plan of reading. In fact, a great deal of their impressive scholarship was incoherent and sometimes superficial, but it served to give them an excellent opinion of their own capacities and to dissatisfy them even more with the aimless existence imposed on them by this egoistic and tyrannical tutor.

For Trophimovsky had definite plans for the children's future. He was the owner of an extensive property and had no intention of letting it go unexploited. This intellectual had the instincts of a peasant, and the cunning, but none of the common sense. He made complicated plans for the development of the grounds, called in experts on horticulture and garden-planning and drew up budgets. Little by little he expected to bring the whole of the jungle-like garden into production and imagined himself living richly off his land. The main expense of such a project would be the hiring of sufficient labour, but Trophimovsky had no intention of paying a penny when he had five tall, strong children growing up around him. The de Moerders were to be his gardeners, and it was thus that none of them was ever allowed to take up a profession or to leave the villa.

It seems extraordinary that the young people should have submitted to such a state of affairs once they had passed the age of adolescence, or that their mother should have permitted it. One can only suppose that Trophimovsky terrorized the entire family, for there is no doubt that his step-children bitterly resented their situation. All of them were weak in character, hesitating, ill-adapted to the realities of life. Their tutor's influence helped to turn them into the poor-spirited creatures they no doubt were, but some disastrous heredity must have been handed down the de Moerder line to produce the neurotic instability that became more and more evident in them as they grew up and which produced the catastrophes that marked their later lives.

The de Moerders hated Vava, as they called Trophimovsky, because he turned them, to all intents and purposes, into agricultural slaves, and they resented his tyranny all the more because they despised him at the bottom of their hearts as a commoner. All of them were extremely conscious of their aristocratic origin and dreamed, like their mother, of the brilliant roles they, as the children of a General in the Tsar's Imperial Army, might have played in the world. On the other hand, they considered that their intellectual attainments fitted them for better things than digging and hoeing. However, there was no reasoning with Trophimovsky when his interests were in cause, and the rare visitors to the house became used to seeing the young people—all of them tall, well-built, fair-haired, with round faces and typically Slav features—busy at their tasks in a garden that none of their efforts seemed to reduce to order.

The spiritual regime at the villa contributed to enervating the three young men, for the household lived according to the principles of the nihilist creed. Everything was subjected to critical examination. What their compatriot, Peter Kropotkin—himself in exile in Geneva—called 'the conventional lies of civilization', were allowed no place inside its walls. The frailties of human nature were sternly set aside, for the ex-pope's criterion was perfection. False sensibility was anathema to him, and to him all sensibility was false. He strove to eradicate it from their nature, with a singular lack of success, and explained to them that love was a mere combination of physical sensations that could be analysed and explained by the laws of physiology. He hated weakness of any kind and made no secret of his contempt for his step-sons, ruthlessly

16

ISABELLE EBERHARDT, AGED 18

THE GARDEN OF THE VILLA NEUVE, MEYRIN, NEAR
GENEVA

crushing their incipient ambitions and impressing on them incessantly that they were good for nothing. It is hardly surprising that they came to believe him, at least in the bottom of their hearts, or that they did their best to compensate for this intimate sentiment of their own inferiority by attaching an inflated importance to their noble birth.

Trophimovsky was, in fact, a terrible tyrant, with a gift for making everyone around him miserable, but he was not perhaps quite such an unscrupulous individual as the indignant neighbours believed. His attachment to his ageing mistress and adopted children was sincere, and his own daughter Isabelle—who resented him as much as any of her brothers during her girlhood—testified later that his intentions had always been good. He was avaricious, but never denied his family anything but their right to freedom. Life treated him hardly. He who habitually ended his letters with the oriental salutation, 'Soyez heureux!' (Be happy!) found no happiness in the Villa Neuve and created none. He had an intransigent spirit which should have been exercised in solitude. In family life it could only sow disaster.

Nathalie was the first to escape. She was a beautiful girl, fair, pale and slender like her mother, and she seems to have had more character than any of the other de Moerders. One day a young man came to the house, sent from the office of a lawyer with whom Trophimovsky had dealings. His name was Jules Perez-Moreyra and his parents were simple people of the lowest rank of the *petite bourgeoisie*—small shopkeepers or humble employees. The young de Moerders found him pleasant company; he returned to the villa in company with his sister and amused himself with the boys while little Marie played with Isabelle in the nursery.

No one noticed his interest in the beautiful Nathalie until she suddenly announced that they were engaged. Then there broke out such storms as even the Villa Neuve had never yet known. Trophimovsky alternated terrible rages with icy sarcasm, inquiring how she expected to live on the wages of an underpaid clerk. His opposition was based entirely on financial grounds and was perhaps stimulated by the fact that Nathalie, on her marriage, would gain control of a small sum left in trust for her by her father. The de Moerders' hostility was quite as vigorous, since they considered that such a plebeian alliance would set the seal on their own social decadence. Madame de Moerder wept, so did the brothers, but Nathalie was not to be moved. Probably she felt that the life of a poverty-stricken little housewife in Geneva was preferable to the disorder and insecurity of the Villa Neuve. At any rate, she married her Jules in 1888, and in so doing cut herself off completely from her family. Her name was never mentioned again, at least in public, and, in spite of an intervention by distant relations in Paris to whom she had appealed, she was never received at the Villa Neuve. Her little sister Isabelle was eleven years old at the time and was less moved than her elders by the event, but she evidently shared the family point of view since, years later, when she described her childhood, she was in the habit of transforming the lawyer's clerk into a Russian officer.

Chapter Two

WHILE the brothers and sisters were already grown-up, Isabelle was undergoing in her turn the dangerous though stimulating influence of Trophimovsky. Her father had early detected in her a quality of mind that was lacking in the weak-spirited de Moerders and he was more determined than ever to mould her according to his own views. He adored her in his own way but saw no reason to treat her differently from her brothers. Few of the conventions of the day as to what a young girl should or should not do could resist his ruthless logic. When occasional visitors expressed their surprise at finding Isabelle, her hair cut short and wearing male clothes, chopping wood in the garden, he would ask sternly whether she appeared any less frail than the young men or any less capable than they of doing such work.

There was really no answer, since she was nearly as tall as they and, although slender, of remarkably robust build. As for her clothes, they were chosen because they were practical. No nihilist, however unmilitant, would admit that a girl might deck herself out with the false seduction that is in itself a lie; and back in Russia the first act of any young woman adhering to the creed would be to put off her pretty clothes, cut off her hair, and don a simple dark frock which could not be suspected as an aid to coquetry. Moreover, men's clothes, according to Trophimovsky, gave 'more security when she goes into town'. The dangers of an excursion into Geneva would not seem to have been great, but he was mistrustful by nature and on principle.

Her education was as complete as that of her brothers, for Trophimovsky taught her the classical languages from an early age, and she could read French, German, Italian, Russian and Arabic. French, indeed, was the language generally used among the de Moerders, as among most Russians of good family at that time, and only the ex-pope remained faithful to his native tongue. She learned from him history, geography and the elements of philosophy, and spent a good deal of her spare time painting and drawing with unusual talent, and certainly better than her father, whose occasional artistic outbreaks were of monstrous size, unhappy design and apt to spread over walls and doors.

Isabelle completed her own education by wide and indiscriminate reading, guided by her favourite brother and next-in-age, Augustin. Her taste in literature, from an early age, was romantic and sentimental, with a preference for the exotic. An early favourite was *Le Roman d'un Spahi* with its purple pictures of desert life. It was followed by all the other works of Pierre Loti, those of d'Annunzio, of Dostoyevsky. She was an enthusiastic admirer of the Russian poet, Nadson, with his rather vague philosophy and the prestige of an early death, and she discovered Baudelaire a little later. Already she was drawn to the sombre and the tragic, seeking perhaps the echo of the disquietude and sad premonitions which were already closing in on her.

As an adolescent, Isabelle had a childish passion for dressing-up and being photographed. One portrait shows her in the outfit of a Spahi—cloak, fez, boots and sash—looking very pleased with herself. Another, taken a little earlier, shows her as a sailor, with the ribbon of the *Vengeur* round her beret.

Then there is Isabelle as a Syrian, Isabelle as a Bedouin. All of these portraits have a quality of slightly equivocal masquerade. The tall, awkward frame, the cropped hair and the masculine clothes are belied by enormous, soft black eyes and the delicate, sensual lips of an awakening woman. The round face, jutting cheek-bones and flat, upturned nose, are those of a Slav peasant; the long, fine hands, those of an aristocrat. The figure in those old photographs seems to be asking herself: 'What am I?'

Perhaps the secret of Isabelle's extreme unhappiness during her early youth lay in this uncertainty about herself. Evasion, movement, liberty were as essential to her as food and drink, and without them she was reduced to unreality. All her references to her own adolescence show that it was a time of continual suffering, not so much on account of material circumstances—since she was loved and spoiled by her entire family —but because her dependence on others compelled her to be incompletely herself, and this, for a nature such as hers, was the most terrible of constraints.

In spite of her love for her mother and Augustin, and the half-unwilling affection that bound her to Trophimovsky, the Villa Neuve was a prison. Perhaps it was the effect of that atmosphere of 'dreary moral nihilism', which the old philosopher created around him, for she wrote later that to fall into such a state was the worst misfortune that could overcome any human being. Its results on the inhabitants of the house were unmistakable. Madame de Moerder, annihilated by the tyranny of her companion, was a timid faded woman who still showed a trace of her old beauty and was loved by all her children for her gentleness and fragility. Vladimir was little more than an unhappy ghost, wandering from room to room, hiding his despair from the world and caring for nothing but the rearing of cactus plants. He had made one fruitless attempt after another to escape. He had begged friends and neighbours to find him a situation, had applied to a well-known florist in Geneva; but the terrible step-father had forestalled every move, and now he was resigned and would make no further effort. Augustin, weak and undecided, knew himself to be hopelessly unadapted to life and took a querulous pride in his unadaptation, and Nicolas, who played so little part in the history of this family, must have resembled him in many ways.

As soon as Isabelle entered the gates of the villa, she was assailed by a feeling of morbid oppression and helplessness. Even the heavy, tropical scent of the plants and flowering shrubs, even the ceaseless singing of the nightingales during the long summer evenings, everything to which she would look back in later days with such sweet nostalgia, only increased her longing for freedom. It was not enough to leave the house and set off along the long, white road that led away into the Jura Mountains. That was only a poor substitute for freedom, since she must return. Trophimovsky had taught her to ride at an early age and she would take her horse, ride up into the hills with a mounting exaltation in her heart, till she was far from any house or the sight of any human being. Then she would tell herself that she was free, in face of the unknown, and she would recognize herself for what she was:

'I was a nomad when, as a little girl, I used to dream and watch the road, the white road that seemed to draw me along it and that wound away, beneath a sun that seemed to me more than naturally brilliant, straight into the delicious inknown. . . . And I shall remain a nomad all my life, in love with changing horizons and unexplored distances. . . .'

This she wrote years later, when the unknown had come to mean for her the Absolute, the face of God, of those expeditions from which she must always return into everyday life. The imagination roamed far beyond those great mountain ranges, but Geneva—'the accursed town' as she dramatically called it—represented unrelenting Reality. It was not enough to adopt the defiant device, *Ibo singulariter donec transeam*—I go on my way alone: the fancy-dress, the passionate exchange of letters with unknown correspondents, the rides into an illusive freedom, could be no more than symbols of an impossible escape to unknown lands.

Occasionally some of the Russian students in Geneva used to visit the Villa Neuve to discuss the situation in Russia, exchange the latest news from St. Petersburg or Moscow and argue over the doctrine of violence, Bakunin's exclusion from the party, or the possibility of setting up an anarchist state, without Army, Church or Law. If Trophimovsky was there, he would smile sceptically in his beard or stump out of the room, according to his mood, for he had little patience with the enthusiasms of youth. Augustin, and perhaps the other brothers, discussed, applauded and planned for themselves energetic and spectacular roles for which they were by nature quite unsuited.

Isabelle herself might have been more tempted by the company of her compatriots if they had not been a part of the life of Geneva. These ardent young men and women were no more exotic to her than the stolid natives of the town, part of the detested everyday life. Her imagination was occupied in far other lands.

In her girlhood, Isabelle had understood the possibilities inherent in pen friendships. The first was with a sailor, probably a chance acquaintance of Augustin, met while on leave from his ship. The letters exchanged between them soon became intimate and sentimental. Then Isabelle noticed one day an announcement in the advertisement columns of a French newspaper:

'Young officer, stationed in the Sahara, bored to death, seeks correspondent.'

The young man's name was Eugène Letord, a lieutenant attached to the Arab Bureau in South Constantine. Isabelle felt that the East was practically on her doorstep and plunged whole-heartedly into a passionate correspondence which, on her side, was largely composed of the wildest fantasies. She signed her letters 'Nadia', gave accounts of herself and her family which varied from week to week, quoted Pierre Loti by the page and poured out philosophic speculations, mingled with irreverent comments, in student's slang, on the life of Geneva.

Eugène Letord was bewildered and intrigued. He was a well-brought-up young man who had no experience of such unorthodox and unpredictable characters, but he soon found 'Nadia' far more interesting than the little French bourgeoise with whom he had expected to exchange reticent letters. She was avid for every detail he could give on the life of the Sahara and he did his best to satisfy her. Luckily for her, he was an observant young man, who was more interested in the life and customs of the natives than his superiors thought necessary for a French officer. He knew that he was considered in the garrison, at the best as an eccentric, at the worst almost as a traitor, and the hostility of his own comrades made the long exile yet harder. He was isolated, unhappy. Isabelle soon became for him, not only a link with Europe, but a comrade with whom he could share his ideas, explain his misgivings over the arrogant methods of colonization which distressed him because they denied the universal brotherhood of man. He and Isabelle spoke the same language. She confided to him her loneliness and unhappiness, told him of Augustin, who suffered as she did in the abnormal atmosphere of the Villa Neuve, who thought only of escape and whose absence she imagined with dread.

Eugène replied, urging the brother and sister to establish themselves in Bône or Algiers, where he had many friends and where he could do much to make their life agreeable. Isabelle took fire at once. She and Augustin dreamed, planned and read all the books they could find that treated of the East. Trophimovsky knew Arabic, among many other languages, and she soon learned from him enough to read parts of the Koran in the original. Its simple, poetic teachings delighted her and she, who had been brought up to despise Christianity, soon began to take a more than intellectual interest in the doctrines of Islam.

It must have been about this time that Isabelle made the acquaintance of the young diplomat of Armenian origin, named Rehid Bey, to whom she gave the name of Archivir. He was attached to the Turkish Consulate in Geneva, and frequented the circle of Russian students in the town—an attractive man, highly cultivated, a lover of poetry, a dreamer, with a nature at once melancholy and violent. He was a devoted Moslem and was enchanted to discover in Isabelle a pupil who asked nothing better than to be initiated in his creed. They discussed philosophy and literature, and Archivir, who believed in the value of physical sensation as a stage on the road to spiritual perfection, probably made love to her in a more or less pressing manner.

The ardent Isabelle needed no more encouragement. She was in love, desperately, hopelessly, and all Vava's sermons and her nihilist comrades' rejection of sentimentality could not hold her back. The old philosopher had failed with her as he failed with the rest of his family, for no amount of lecturing could constrain a nature so essentially romantic and sensual. As for Archivir, he was not inclined to take a seventeen-year-old student very seriously and he was probably a little alarmed at the passion he had aroused. He changed his mind in a few years' time, but by then it was to be too late.

Luckily, there was Augustin in whom she could always find comfort and encouragement. The elder brother listened, encouraged and admired. They shared all their hopes and plans and vowed to each other never to part. They would go for immense walks together, climbing the dusty road to Collanges, up to the first mountain range of the Haute Savoie; or else cross the French frontier beyond Bellegarde, and reach the spot where the road overlooked the majestic valley of the Rhone; or else wander by the lake, watching the little sailing boats drifting across from France and anchoring by the quiet Quai de Paquis. They would talk interminably, making plans for distant voyages. Isabelle dreamed of Istanbul, without explaining the attraction she felt for the town. Then they talked of Mecca and the great pilgrimage to the holy centre of Islam, to which no infidel might have access; then of Algiers, and the home in its Casbah, which Eugène Letord described so invitingly and in which they imagined passing their lives together, dreaming and studying and travelling in the desert.

Augustin agreed to everything, swept away by his sister's enthusiasm. He agreed, indeed, with anything anyone suggested to him—with Isabelle when she proposed marvellous journeys, with the anarchists who sought to enrol him in their activities, and, above all, with Trophimovsky, who preached the futility of action. He hated his step-father's tyranny but allowed himself to be impregnated with his philosophy. The walks and discussions with Isabelle, long arguments with the Russian colony, with whom he was always more or less in discord, and quarrels with Trophimovsky, were for a long time the sum of his existence.

Yet, inactive as he was by nature, Augustin was not wholly resigned to so meaningless a life and was beginning to seek dangerous distractions from the ennui of existence at Meyrin. Gradually his contacts with the anarchist milieu became closer, involving him with strange people and in strange doings.

Geneva at this period was the home of innumerable revolutionaries who had fled from their homelands to the shelter of tolerant and hospitable Switzerland. The Russians were the most numerous and the most conspicuous. They were supported by the ever-increasing movement in their own land where, in spite of wholesale deportations to Siberia, revolutionary doctrines were sweeping through the universities. They were convinced of the necessity for terrorism. Active and ardent, they dedicated their lives to the overthrow of the Tsarist regime and believed in political assassination as an essential weapon. Alexander II had been killed by a nihilist a few years earlier and the Empress Elizabeth of Austria was to die at the hands of an Italian anarchist three years later. The police were uneasy; the population was beginning to view with dislike the cosmopolitan crowd of hungry-looking refugees that thronged into the country and were suspected of being behind the strikes, the political upheavals and the subversive journals like *L'Egalité*, *Le Progrès* and *Le Révolté* which were slipped under the doors of respectable business men and contained inflammatory appeals to the workers, attacked Christianity and the Army and denounced all political authority as evil in itself.

The Russian colony was particularly mysterious and disquieting. Its members lived in cheap furnished rooms—four or five to a room—in the poorest quarters or in obscure suburbs. They visited each other, cooked frugal meals in common and talked endlessly. Some were students, living on so little money that their existence seemed almost a miracle, working with fanatic determination for the degrees which would enable them to return to their own country and to pursue their work among the poor and disinherited with greater efficiency. They were so poor that a whole group would sometimes possess only one decent suit and each would take his turn at attending the day's lectures, clothed in this communal garment and taking copious notes for the instruction of the comrades who awaited him at home. Some lived by giving lessons; some received tiny subsidies from clandestine organizations at home. All were in some degree conspirators and propagandists. Delegates were dispatched back to Russia from time to time, charged to kill certain notorious agents of the reaction. Sometimes they succeeded, but the Tsarist police was watchful and its agents well-informed. In any case, it was rare for these delegates to return alive and there were rumours in Geneva of romantic last gatherings in the attics around the Bourg-du-Four, where the funeral dirge of the appointed martyr would be sung before he took a final leave of his comrades.

Little by little, Augustin had come into closer contact with these revolutionaries and managed to gain their confidence and to enrol among them. No doubt he never understood that they were in earnest and that he was playing with fire. He seems to have been mixed up at the same time in a number of doubtful transactions and especially to have frequented a group of people who not only drugged themselves but procured and sold opium and other products. The drug and the excitement of his political activities kept him in a continual state of emotional crisis. Isabelle was his only confidante and his family were kept in complete ignorance.

The events of 1894 remain mysterious. It seems that Augustin took fright, perhaps betrayed his comrades, was certainly involved in some financial scandal. He had debts which he dared not avow to Trophimovsky; a love affair of which his family certainly disapproved tormented his overstrained nerves yet further and drove him to continual hysterical outbursts. The atmosphere at the Villa Neuve was appalling and Isabelle, who alone knew part of the truth, was its chief victim. Then one day Augustin and Nicolas disappeared and inquiries in the town showed that Augustin's little fiancée, Madeleine Joliet, was also gone from her home.

Isabelle seems to have been behind the flight and to have urged Augustin to escape from some impending, unspecified disaster. In spite of her brother's five-year seniority, it was she who planned, lectured and urged reason. Perhaps her own over-heated imagination—for Augustin seems to have initiated her into the use of stimulants—exaggerated the danger from Russia, yet subsequent events suggest that her fears were not entirely unfounded. At any rate, she decided that Augustin must leave Geneva and enlist in the French Navy, in company with a young sailor whom they had met during one of his leaves and with whom they had remained in close relation. The departure was to be organized in such a way as to avoid rousing Trophimovsky's suspicions or causing too much pain to her mother, but Augustin was by now incapable of reasoned action and his departure was a crazy flight that could only make the worst of a tangled and unsavoury situation.

Isabelle herself had no idea of his whereabouts. Between the furious Trophimovsky and a terrorized, broken-hearted mother, she lived weeks of agony. Augustin had been her one love, the one reason for her existence. Now he had abandoned her without a word and revelation after revelation of his foolishness and lack of scruple came to overwhelm her. She hid all that she could from her parents but could not prevent them from learning of certain debts that were serious

28

enough to be almost fraudulent. Trophimovsky forbade her to have anything more to do with her brother, but could not prevent her from using every means in her power to track him down. A few clandestine letters arrived for her at the Poste Restante at Vernier, but they were vague and neither gave an address nor revealed his intentions. She wrote to friends, made inquiries in the Navy, enlisted the help of Madeleine Joliet's sister, traced the couple to the Savoy and then to Corsica. Nicolas was suddenly, inexplicably in Russia, and the extraordinary imbroglio became deeper than ever. Had he betrayed his brother and his comrades, sold the secrets of the anarchist society, or fallen a victim himself to the Tsar's secret police? The family seems to have regarded him later as a traitor and held him responsible for their misfortunes.

Then, in the autumn, when the fallen leaves lay thick over the great garden, Isabelle received news from an old comrade to whom she had applied for help and who informed her that her brother was at Sidi-bel-Abbès in North Africa. Augustin, the weak, the undecided, the beloved, had joined the Foreign Legion. He had signed an engagement for five years and for five unending years they were to be parted.

Her first reaction was a mixture of fury and despair. Augustin had ignored her advice, plunged them all into fear and anxiety. In this household of feeble neurotics, Isabelle felt herself responsible. She wrote immediately, pouring out her rage and misery in an immense letter, scrawled on foolscap pages torn from an exercise book.

'This evening I have just received a letter from Vivicorsi in which, in answer to one of mine signed N. Podilinsky, sailor (I did not know how else to win his confidence) he informs me that you have joined the Legion. It is as if I had been struck by thunder. What have you done! ! ! What have you done, wretch! Have you gone completely mad and are you not even aware of what you are doing? I am in complete despair. Nobody knows anything as yet. *Impossible to mention this letter.* And what is the meaning of all this incoherence? What were you doing in Savoy? What were you doing on the Neos Georgios, and at Toulon, and at Marseilles? Why did you write that you were going to South America? Why, finally, did you not join the Navy by some means or another?

'You must have gone absolutely mad! And do you not understand the terrible results of what you have done, wretch?

'This evening there seems to be no limit to my despair. What have you done, my God! my God!

'No, really, I no longer have any idea what to do. I am done for this evening, absolutely done for. Everything is finished for me. No, no, life has become impossible. All of you, whom I have loved so much, and loved to the point of folly, are killing me.

'Even without this new affair, my life has been absolutely destroyed by the terrible things that have happened here.

'Still, I must resign myself, I must try to write something else than the terrible cries of pain that are wrung from me by this wound in my heart. Try to write? What is the use? What is the use? Yet I must force myself to say the things which it is my duty to say to you:

'You must write here! Write! Yet the only things you have to tell them are so awful and so miserable. But I formally forbid you to write to me before you have written to *Mama*, only to *her*. I shall curse you if you do not do so. You will end by killing her. You *must* write, or the old people will go completely mad.

'Write for how long you have joined up. I vaguely understand the mad, mad, mad plan that has grown up in your inflamed brain: obtain your naturalization through the Legion, then enter the *State*.[1]

'Isn't that it? Well, is it not the plan of a visionary and a madman? *Five years of what?* Then, the Navy! After five years in Africa or in Tonkin! You are lost. And by losing yourself, you have lost me, completely lost me. I had put my last hope

[1] All soldiers of the French Foreign Legion were eligible for naturalization after completing five years' service.

in you and now everything is finished. I do not know what to do, or what to think.

'No, no, there is no more hope for me in this damned life of eternal darkness.

'And the only thing I can do to save myself from this insupportable pain. . . . I *must* not do it! But how long shall I be able to hold out?'

Almost at the same time, a brief letter reached her from Augustin himself, confirming the news:

Sidi-bel-Abbès,
12th November 1894.

My beloved.

Augustin de Moerder, soldier in the 1st Foreign Regiment, 18th Company, no. 19686, at Sidi-bel-Abbès, near Oran (Algeria).

There, my beloved, lies the whole sad truth. Yet I think of you, of Mama, of Vava. And I tell myself once more: Hieme et aestate, et prope et procul, usque dum vivam et ultra.

Believe me, your
Augustin.

In face of this catastrophe, Isabelle realized the depth of her need and love for Augustin. Nothing else could count for her, not even Archivir, nothing could comfort her for this unbearable absence. Vava, 'the old thinker', attempted comfort in his own way. He had always had a poor opinion of his stepsons and knew Isabelle to be made of better and sterner stuff. He forbade her to write to the erring brother, whose creditors were assailing him and driving him nearly frantic with rage. The mother, on the other hand, lived in a perpetual flood of tears and would have done anything to have news of the absent son, while Isabelle's only consolation was to write immensely long letters and receive occasional replies at the Poste Restante.

Her anger with Augustin could not last, and on Christmas Eve, after weeks of misery, she retired to her room and poured out her loneliness and longing in a letter, peppered with exclamation marks and quotations in Greek, Latin and Arabic, which is more like that of a lover than of a sister:

'The weather is sad and grey, the earth covered with snow. To-night, my beloved, I am sending you from Vernier the memories of my unhappy heart. I shall be away from the house most of the night, for I am going alone, with our old servant, to the midnight mass at the Catholic church. . . . It is the first time, my beloved, that we have been separated for this festival, separated perhaps for Time and for Eternity! Who knows if we shall ever meet again? Who knows whether the kisses exchanged on the doorstep at ten o'clock on October the 12th were not to be our last. We have never been separated for so long. What desolation, what heavy sadness, deep and implacable! There is no hope and no faith. No God to whom we might cry out our nameless pain, all the atrocious injustice of our suffering. Heaven is empty and dumb; there is nothing, no one anywhere. The loneliness is absolute. For us two loneliness is absolute, remember that! Nobody will ever understand our suffering, our hopes and our despair.

'And why must we live separated, far from each other? "My God!" A mechanical phrase! God!

'Where are our make-believes, our hopes, our plans for the future? Oh Tino, those papers that we signed on 21st September 1894 in which we asked ourselves where we should be the following year, what we should be doing and in what and whom we should be placing our hopes? Bottomless mystery of the future! One year and a few days later I find myself alone here, and in such a solitude!

'And you are a soldier out there, in the land of the Maghreb, of Dar-el-Islam, which, you remember, was our holy Kaaba for both of us.

'Do you remember the phrase which concludes "Visions du Maghreb": "Oh, our human souls which last but a day,

ISABELLE EBERHARDT, AGED 19

MANUSCRIPT PAGE FROM A SHORT STORY BY ISABELLE EBERHARDT

Photo kindly lent by M. R. L. Doyon

where will you be to-morrow and where will be your memory?"

'. . . Do you remember that day when we were both seated in the silent valley, in the shade of the white maple trees and the laburnums in the mountains above Collanges? We were alone in the great, eternal silence. . . .

'. . . Oh, to be together once more, in the shadow of the great, silent Credo! But no, no doubt that will never be again! Never! What an abyss of pain in that word: Never, and there is the alpha and omega of all human pain, of all tortures. . . . Everything is sunk in a sort of fog of melancholy, in the mortal fog of the present. When shall we meet again, and shall we ever meet again?

'But you must always trust me, in spite of the distance. . . . And for ever, for it can change nothing.

'I am suffering. The present has no horizon; it is gloomy, shadowy, desolate.

> *My body is in the West*
> *And my heart is in the East;*
> *My body is in the land of the infidel*
> *And my heart is at Stamboul,*
> *And my heart is at Oran! . . .*

'At Stamboul! You know why . . . you surely managed to unravel the truth, the miserable truth, in all that, with our unimaginable characters, I told you about. . . . You were able to understand and guess. Yet that love, that unhappy love which was never returned, was nothing in comparison with the immaterial love I have for you. If Eternity exists, with which of you should I choose to live again. . . ?

'If Eternity exists, with which of the two should I choose to live again elsewhere? With him, my beloved brother, or with you? Oh, with you, always with you! . . .

'Where? Out there, in the Unknowable future of to-morrow, beyond the grave. Oh, let me remain, whatever I may hope for else, always with you.

'And if Eternity exists, these immaterial loves, so deep and

33

inexplicable, must live again with us. . . . Only they can arouse in us that great trembling before the Unknown and the vague presentiment of a *to-morrow*, of a mysterious other world. Only love, the two loves—that which is like our own and that which has been born in me for the brown-eyed Levantine. "Is it the supreme effort of the soul towards heaven or a blind law of nature?"[1]

'But always, always with you, near or far, always.'

Poor Isabelle! The measure of her love was never to be found in its object and her love was never to be bestowed on those who might have been worthy of it. When she found Augustin again, time and space had done their work and he was no longer the beloved companion she had known. As for the brown-eyed Levantine, Rehid Bey, he was to bring her little real happiness and much disillusionment.

Meanwhile, she was kept in constant anxiety by the irrational behaviour of Augustin. After a few weeks of enthusiasm he began to tire of the Legion and to plan for his release. Isabelle, hopeless and miserable without him, yet feared his return more than anything else. She was clear-sighted enough to realize that no disaster could be worse than to take up again the 'useless life' which he had left. She sent him books, urged him to work, to study, to return to a sense of reality.

'You must give up living on visions and fantasies,' she wrote. Then, constantly bearing in mind the danger which— perhaps by prudence—she never specified, she begged him to write to the Emperor of Russia and declare that he had disavowed his nationality, thus safeguarding himself from pursuit for the crimes—presumably political—which he had committed in Geneva.

There was no reasoning with Augustin, however, and he was determined to leave the Legion. Trophimovsky, as impulsive and unreasonable as himself, gradually began to view his behaviour with more leniency and, to Isabelle's horror, began to speak of obtaining his step-son's liberation, bringing

[1] The quotation is from Loti's exotic novel, *Aziyadé*.

him back to Geneva and setting him up as a market gardener. Isabelle dissuaded her brother with difficulty from accepting, but could not prevent him intriguing, with Trophimovsky's help, for a release on the grounds of ill-health. All she could do was to urge him not to return to the dangers of Geneva but to remain in Africa as a colonist.

She was living through a period of unforgettable misery, abandoned in the gloomy house between the increasingly embittered Trophimovsky, a mother crushed by grief and the general difficulty of her existence, and a brother in the throes of acute melancholia. Nothing could distract her, though she bent all her will to save herself from spiritual destruction, forced herself to draw, to paint, to study medicine, and, above all, to write. She wrote of the Orient—the imagined Orient that she loved so much and of which Eugène Letord sent her accounts alternately glowing and despondent. The erudite Archivir vaunted to her the spiritual beauties of Islam and, at her request, put her in touch with several learned Arabs in North Africa and elsewhere with whom she entered into correspondence under a variety of assumed names. She sent them stories and articles for criticism; an old Turk, Abou Naddara, who had known her family in Istanbul and was now editing a journal in Paris, described certain of them as 'sublime'. Soon he was writing to her as 'my dear daughter', urging her to make a literary career for herself and to base it on a study of the East and Arab life. The dream was taking shape. A travelling photographer, an Algerian named Louis David, was touring Switzerland with his wife. They had met Augustin in North Africa and brought news of him to the Villa Neuve, where they became friends of the family. Isabelle confided her unhappiness, her longing for Augustin, her fear that he might return to Geneva, her obsession with the East. The Davids listened sympathetically and proposed a practical solution. They possessed a house in Bône, where life was cheap, easy and delightful, and suggested renting it to Isabelle for as long as she wished to stay.

There remained the problem of her mother. The gentle,

fragile 'White Spirit'—it was by this name, always written in Russian characters, that Isabelle referred to her mother in her diary—could not be left at the mercy of Trophimovsky's increasingly difficult character and Vladimir's recurrent attacks of neurasthenia. It was not difficult to persuade her, for the poor woman was completely exhausted by the constant emotional strain at the villa. The decision was taken and the two women began to prepare their departure. Isabelle, who had dreamed since her early girlhood of *Dar-el-Islam*—the House of Islam—was about to give reality to her dreams and take the first step on the road to her destiny.

They left in the early spring of 1897. The Villa Neuve was now almost deserted, its occupants invisible to the outside world. No one could tell what took place behind those heavy, barred gates, but one day, a few months after the departure of Isabelle and her mother, Trophimovsky wrote a brief letter to the village schoolmistress:

'My cactophile is dead. Come!'

The unhappy Vladimir had closed the key of the stove in his room so that the fumes should put an end to a useless and finally unbearable existence. He died at eleven o'clock in the morning of 13th April 1898. Among the people of Vernier—who were always ready to believe the worst of Trophimovsky—the rumour crept round that his stepfather had suggested the act, perhaps even forced him to it, but no one ever knew the truth.[1]

---

[1] Among the letters left by Trophimovsky which came into Isabelle's hands after his death, is a totally inexplicable one to his bankers in Moscow. In it he refers to 'the two orphans, afflicted by the terrible death of their elder brother, the gentle Vladimir, martyrized by Nicolas de Moerder and by the Russian Consul, the cruel Polish Count Prozov.

'They tortured him on 14th December 1897. The unhappy boy escaped from the hands of the criminals but left his reason there. He was struck down by acute madness, which drove him to commit suicide on April 13th. . . .'

If this letter is based on more than the persecution mania and hallucinations which seem to have been endemic to all the inhabitants of the Villa Neuve—including Isabelle herself—Vladimir must have been involved in the same political activities as Augustin, and was perhaps his scapegoat. The role of Nicolas is even harder to explain.

Chapter Three

BÔNE was a little white town lying on the coast at a point directly south of Sardinia. There was a large European colony which felt itself immeasurably superior to the 'natives', even when a goodly proportion of it was composed of the riff-raff of various north Mediterranean countries, adventurers with doubtful pasts who would have been treated with small consideration in their own lands. The French colony was roughly divided into a few idealists who believed that the imperial grandeur of their land and the interests of the new country might be made to march hand in hand; a certain number of enterprising men, determined to get rich as quickly as possible; and the mass of small, conscientious employees who were only mildly interested in their work and desired to return to France as soon as the financial situation would permit.

This European quarter in no way corresponded to the dreams of Isabelle and her mother, steeped in the sumptuous imagery of Pierre Loti. The prim functionaries, absorbed in small ambitions and respectful of all hierarchies, were even stranger to them than the bourgeoisie of Geneva. Isabelle, impetuous and intolerant, would have nothing to do with their narrow existence. Within a few months she had installed herself with her mother in a house in the rue Bugeaud, near the ancient fort. The Europeans, surprised and resentful, gossiped ill-naturedly and would have ignored the new arrivals if these had noticed that they were being ignored.

The house was built of beaten earth, whitewashed over, with a flat roof that served as a terrace on which to sleep, rolled in a burnous, or to read or to watch the dark blue sea and the thronging boats of the little port. The rooms were probably grouped, in the fashion of the better-class Arab houses, round a small inner courtyard, with a floor of coloured mosaics, and perhaps a little fountain, bordered with miniature orange trees. Within a few minutes' walk was the noisy, careless, unhygienic life of the native quarter—half-naked children with eyelids gnawed away by trachoma tumbling like puppies in the dust and filth; veiled women, swathed like mummies in their black robes, with tinkling ornaments of gold and silver on their arms and foreheads; beggars hung about with nameless rags; tellers of stories and merchants who sold rare perfumes or scraps of tin with the same nonchalance; young effendis wearing the red, tasselled fez, who wandered dreamily, holding each other by the little finger.

Five times a day, from the minaret of every mosque in the town, the voice of the *muezzin* rang out, calling the faithful to prayer. At the first sign of dawn, Isabelle was awakened by the melancholy call of the horn and the long-drawn, plaintive cry, 'Prayer is better than sleep!' which echoed and died across the roof-tops. Then the whole town stirred, and in every home men and women prostrated themselves, their faces towards Mecca, and repeated the great cry of Islam: *Allah Akbar; ashadon an illaha illa lah*—'God is great; I testify that there is no god but God.' And so it continued throughout the day, till at sunset came the last call of the horn and the call to the last prayer: *Hay ala salate, Allah Akbar*—'To prayer, to prayer! God is great.'

Even then the life of the town hardly slackened. The crowds continued to jostle in the narrow streets, to gossip and gamble on the long flights of steps; the pipes continued to wail from the cafés. 'He who closes his eyes often, fears to look on God,' says the old Bedouin proverb, and the people of Bône preferred to spend their nights in gossip, story-telling and the drinking of bitter coffee.

Sometimes, late at night in the maze of lanes so narrow that two men could hardly pass abreast, Isabelle smelt the heavy, penetrating, unmistakable smell of *kif*. A new law had been passed a few years earlier forbidding the use of the drug, and the police patrolled the Casbah at night, sniffing the air for tell-tale whiffs, but it was still smoked in cellars and the back rooms of cafés in ill-famed streets where even they hesitated to enter. The smell intrigued and excited her; she would have liked to share in every custom of the Orient so that she might become really a part of it and throw off even the memory of Europe.

Isabelle had rarely worn women's clothes, and here, in a country where no woman might wander unaccompanied, male Arab dress seemed a natural protection. Soon she was to be seen in the long, snowy-white burnous and the high, swathed muslin turban of an Algerian bourgeois. The Europeans were horrified, but her choice had been made and their opinion was indifferent to her. The Arabs were more tolerant. Her conduct was not unprecedented among unmarried girls. One of the great cheikhs from the South could frequently be seen in Algiers in the company of what appeared to be a slender boy, richly dressed in embroidered cloak and burnous, who walked at his side and sat with him on the terrace of the principal cafés. This was his fifteen-year-old daughter and constant companion. Other young Amazons used to ride in male dress in the desert and take part in spectacular fantasias with the crack horsemen of their tribes, without causing any surprise. Isabelle's behaviour, in the native quarters of Bône and the coastal regions of Tunisia and Algeria, probably caused less surprise than it had in Geneva. In the fanatic South, prejudice was stronger and, as she was to discover, could provoke violent reactions.

In Bône she was received in a way which few Europeans

could have hoped for. She had come to the town with introductions to wealthy and cultivated families. Archivir opened for her doors that would ordinarily have remained closed. So did a distinguished Tunisian functionary named Abd-ul-Wahab, whom her brother had known during his stay in Africa. She herself could offer unusual references. She had learned classical Arabic from Trophimovsky—that is, the written language which, when spoken, is only understood by scholars, but she learned the North African dialect with astonishing ease and could converse freely at the end of a few months. She was learned in matters relating to Islam and Archivir had given her an insight into the Moslem religion which went deeper than a mere acquaintance with the Koran. In fact, she was no ordinary *roumia* and the great families of Bône were delighted to invite her to their homes. She visited them wearing male or female native dress, as the fancy took her, and her slightly equivocal situation did not at all deter some of their sons from making love to her. A rich young Tunisian offered marriage; she was not tempted. Marriage meant taking her place among the women of the Casbah, accepting a condition of inferiority, and, above all, losing her liberty. She had come to Bône with the intention of entering fully into the life of the Orient, but she could never have accepted the condition of a Moslem woman. She refused the Tunisian and continued her independent life.

Isabelle intended to put that life to good account. She had a practical side to her nature and a good deal of ambition. She had already made up her mind to be a writer and decided to make use of her unique opportunities for observing the life of the country for literary purposes. Almost since childhood she had noted her thoughts and comments on her daily life in a series of diaries. Now she began to transpose these observations into short stories. One of these, after passing by a number of versions, satisfied her sufficiently for an attempt at publication. It is called *Yasmina* and tells the story of the love of a simple Bedouin girl for a young French officer and the tragedy this impossible love brings into her life. It is told simply, with such attention to detail and minute observation that the two main characters, who might easily have been the habitual lay figures of romantic exotic literature, take on a life of their own, and their destiny is really human and moving. It is perhaps the most successful of the many stories of Arab life which were discovered after Isabelle's death and published under the title of 'Aux Pays des Sables'.

'Yasmina' was accepted by a local newspaper. When it appeared Isabelle felt more confident than ever that she would be able to follow in the footsteps of her beloved Pierre Loti and make a name for herself in the world of letters. Her diary was filled with documentation to serve as basis for books and stories—brief notes on local customs, word sketches of people or landscapes, hastily noted as a painter might make a swift sketch to be used later as the material for a picture. Sometimes, too, there were actual sketches, neatly and fairly skilfully executed in pen and ink or in pencil—a house like a cube pierced by a low door, the rounded cupola of a mosque, the interior of some home where she had been invited to sip coffee and smoke with an acquaintance.

Isabelle's literary ambitions, however, still remained on the surface of her life. To Abd-ul-Wahab she wrote:

'Perhaps you have guessed that for me the ambition to "make a name and a position for myself" by my pen (a thing in which I have little confidence and cannot even hope to attain) is quite secondary. I write because I like the "processus" of literary creation; I write, in the same way as I love, because it is my destiny, probably. And it is my only real consolation.'

And again, in another letter to the same attentive friend, she spoke of the task which she had set herself and for the accomplishment of which her writing was always to be an instrument rather than an end in itself:

'There are things in me which I do not understand yet or am only just beginning to understand, and there are a great many such mysteries. Yet I study myself as hard as I can; I spend all my energy in putting into practice the aphorism of the Stoics: "Know yourself." It is a difficult task, seductive

and painful. The thing which does me most harm is the prodigious mobility of my character and the deplorable instability
of my moods, which succeed each other with incredible
rapidity. I suffer from it and I know of no other remedy than
the silent contemplation of nature, far from mankind, face to
face with the great Inconceivable, the only refuge of distressed souls.'

Isabelle was a natural mystic, but her conversion to Islam
seems to have been made largely for practical reasons. Her
absorption in her new life was too great to allow her to remain contented with the rôle of a favoured outsider.

Her acquaintances were many and hospitable, but it could
not have been long before she perceived that however freely
she might be accepted in certain emancipated Arab homes,
there was an impassable barrier between herself and the inner
life of the Casbah. Whatever favours her Arab dress and
knowledge of the language might win her, she was an infidel,
branded with the mark of the Christianity she had been taught
to hate. The acceptation of Islam was easy to her. Archivir
had prepared the way. The old pope had brought her up in
the doctrine of fatalism, which is, indeed, natural to the Slav
character. Islam gave a meaning to fatalism. Constantly on
the lips of her friends she heard the word 'Mektoub'—'it is
written'. Everything is written beforehand and the irrevocable destiny of each individual is the will of God.

The conversations of the Arabs, their stories, their proverbs,
were full of this idea of submission to one's destiny. The wise
old men, as they puffed at their pipes, illustrated this conception in a hundred different ways. Sometimes they went back
to the creation of the world.

'As soon as God had created the pen,' they recounted, 'He
said to it: Write!

'And the pen asked: O Lord, what shall I write?

'God replied: Write down the destiny of all things, to the
end of the world.

'And the pen wrote down everything that is, and everything that is to be, until the end of time.'

Then they would recite the fifth commandment of Mohammed: 'Attribute everything to God, because everything comes from Him. Let your resignation be such that if Good and Bad Luck were transformed into two horses and you were offered your choice of a mount, you would leap without hesitation on to the back of that which was nearest, without seeking to know which it was. Since both Good and Bad Luck are sent by God, it is not for you to make a choice.'

In all Isabelle's writings—her notes, her diaries and her stories—this sense of the unescapable destiny of mankind appears and reappears like a recurring motif. She found in it a sort of refuge. To resign herself to the will of God—or to destiny—was a sort of acceptance of her own nature.

'The only consolation to be found for me,' she wrote a little later, 'lies in my increasing Moslem *resignation*. . . . At last I can discover in my heart the beginning of that indifference towards indifferent people and things which is the strongest affirmation of myself.'

And constantly, reading over her diaries year after year and meditating on the gap between projects made and the realization brought by life, she made notes in the margin:

'God wrote nothing here.'

'So far, God has written nothing.'

The way to Islam is made easy, especially to a woman. It is sufficient to raise the right hand and recite with a sincere heart, in the presence of two witnesses, the formula of belief:

Achadou an la ilaha illallah wa Mohammadan rasoul Allah —'I bear witness that there is no god but God and Mohammed is his prophet.'

One day, in the home of some pious but broad-minded friends, Isabelle, in company with her mother, made her declaration of faith. She was joined now, for ever, to Islam and she was to find in the religion of Mohammed the one consolation in a continually tragic life.

The first episode of that tragedy occurred barely a year after her installation at Bône. Nathalie de Moerder, the 'White Spirit', had suffered for some time from a disease of the heart.

The agitated life at the Villa Neuve, the shock of Augustin's flight, the uprooting from Geneva had aggravated her condition. On 28th November 1897 she succumbed to a heart attack. Her death certificate names her as 'Nathalie Korff, aged 59, born at St. Petersburg, daughter of Nicolas Korff and —'. The blank must have stood for the German mother, the Lutheran and erring Fraulein Eberhardt, in whose name she had contracted her marriage. She was buried in the name of Fatma, which she had taken on her conversion, in the Moslem cemetery on the hill overlooking the harbour, where the tombs of white marble and coloured china seemed like brilliant flowers among the great black cypress trees, the virginia creeper, the giant geraniums and the Berber *kerams*.

Isabelle's grief at her mother's death was as violent and excessive as it had been two years earlier at the desertion of Augustin. Trophimovsky, summoned in haste but arriving too late to bid farewell to his companion, found his daughter in a state of frenzied despair. The old nihilist himself showed no sign of what he might be feeling. He had little sympathy for human weaknesses, and when Isabelle, weeping and distraught, cried out that she was determined to die and rejoin her beloved mother, he calmly offered her his revolver. Isabelle's courage failed her, as he must have known it would. She regained a measure of calm, and when the brief funeral was accomplished it was the ex-pope who broke down and fell weeping to the ground.

Isabelle never forgot her mother. Almost to the day of her death she continued to recall her, with infinite longing, in her private diaries. Two years later, in Cagliari, the bitter pain of that separation had not yet been calmed.

'How can I keep any illusions,' she wrote one day of profound sadness, 'when the white dove who was the sweetness and light of my life is sleeping out there in the earth, in the quiet cemetery, among the Faithful of Anneba?'[1]

The last person who had exercised some measure of restraint over her had disappeared. From now on, Isabelle was

[1] Bône.

surrendered by the *Mektoub* to her own contradictory and
excessive nature. She was twenty years old and very sure of
herself. A few years later, when she had gained in lucidity, she
was to sum herself up with remarkable detachment:

'If the strangeness of my life were the result of snobbishness
or posing, people might be able to say: She brought it on
herself! But that is not the case; no one ever lived more from
day to day and more according to hazard than I do. It is the
inexorable chain of events that has led me to this point and
not I who have created those events. Perhaps the strangeness
of my nature may be summed up in one characteristic—the
seeking for new events, at whatever cost, and the flight from
inaction and immobility.'

From now on, nothing could hold her back. She was
launched on that life of an eternal wanderer whose need of
incessant movement was stronger than any other impulse.
The demon of change had taken possession and was to keep
her in his clutches until the last day, when the raging waters
of Ain Sefra would bring her flight to an end.

Chapter Four

A few months later the people of Tunis, Europeans and Arabs alike, were beginning to gossip about the scandalous life of a young woman who had taken up her quarters in the Casbah. She was commonly supposed to be a Jewess of Polish origin, although she gave herself out as the daughter of a Russian Moslem married to a German Lutheran. She herself belonged to the faith of this alleged father and practised assiduously the rites of the Islamic religion, although, like many town-dwelling Arabs, she ignored the Prophet's rule against the drinking of alcohol. She dressed and lived as a man, refusing to acknowledge the right of either European or Moslem society to place the slightest check on her personal freedom.

She was generally to be seen clad in a long burnous, her head covered by a turban or a fez, stretched out on a mat of woven palm in one of the innumerable native cafés. Sometimes she would lie there, lethargic as the laziest Arab in the Casbah, smoking cigarettes endlessly and dreaming from dawn till dusk. Sometimes she seemed to be filled with an almost frenzied energy, interpellating passers-by, calling out pleasantries in a harsh nasal voice, wrestling with the red-cloaked young Spahis whom she usually managed to overcome, for she was taller than most of them and remarkably strong.

At other times she was to be found in the homes of rich Tunisians, discussing the Koran with the old men or allowing the young ones to make love to her as the fancy took them. More often she was in the outskirts of the town, wandering, under the disguise of a Bedouin nomad, in the lonely cemetery of Bab-el-Gorjani, or else in the slum quarters where the very poor lived in crumbling huts of beaten mud, clad in verminous rags and nourished on whatever horrid scraps luck might bring their way. The Europeans wondered what she found to do there, and the authorities, listening to the reports that circulated among the residents, asked themselves whether this stranger, whose accounts of herself varied according to her humour of the moment, might not be an agent of the English, sent to stir up resentment against an administration which did little to ameliorate the lot of the natives. It seemed the only plausible explanation of the preference she showed for the company of the most disinherited, poorest and dirtiest section of the Arab population, rather than their own. She was watched; agents in the native quarters reported that she led a dissolute life but that her piety was beyond question and that she never failed to recite the ritual prayers, prostrated towards Mecca, five times a day. Islam places little sexual restraint on men and this woman chose—for this very reason, said evil tongues—to consider herself as a man. At any rate, her religion gave her access to circles where she could do most harm. Contempt for an eccentric began to give way to a certain uneasiness.

Yet those who despised and rejected Isabelle on moral grounds might have been astonished if they had known how much of her life was spent in meditation, dreaming and solitude. She had taken an old house in a deserted corner of Bab-Menara, built in the Turkish style with a labyrinth of winding passages, the rooms all on different levels, decorated with ancient tiles of multi-coloured china or sculptured plaster that

47

fringed the domed ceilings of gilded wood. Often she would pass whole days in the cool dusk of these rooms, in the sole company of her servant, a very old ex-slave named Khadija, and Dédale, her fierce black dog. No sound pierced the thick walls save the faint call of the *meuzzin*, nor could the most stifling heat penetrate into the huge room, lined with pink and green tiles, where she lay smoking the bemusing *kif* and noting the impressions of her excursions into the town.

At the back of the house lay a huddle of ruined houses, with little courtyards, terraces and crumbling arches, all smothered in virginia creeper, invading grass and hardy flowers peeping among the cracks of the masonry. There was one courtyard in particular that fascinated Isabelle because it was so exquisite and so lonely. It was surrounded by the remnants of the walls of houses that had never been inhabited in living memory. In the centre there was a stone fountain that was still full of limpid water that rose from some hidden source. It was paved with snow-white tiles and its walls were almost hidden behind bushes of crimson roses and heavy-scented jasmine.

Once every month a stranger used to appear in this deserted garden, a young Moor, light-skinned, of extraordinary beauty and dressed in flowing draperies of faded silk. He would seat himself on a stone near the fountain, take a little flute from his pocket and play gravely, with an air of ineffable melancholy, the frail monotonous tunes of ancient Arab songs. Then he would sing, apparently unaware of any audience, and when his song was finished go away as silently and mysteriously as he had come.

Isabelle came to expect his monthly visit and would watch for him from behind the iron trellis of her window. One day she noted one of his songs. It went:

'My sorrow devours my soul as the night devours my heart and fills it with anguish, as the tomb devours the corpse and annihilates it. There is no cure for my sadness except irrevocable death. But if my soul awakes to another life, even if it should be in Eden, my sorrow would awake with it.'

But when Isabelle called Khadija and showed her the

strange young man, the old woman shivered and declared that he belonged to none of the great families of the town but was certainly an apparition from the dead and his music a powerful spell.

Arab courtesy forbade the questioning of a stranger, and one month the visitor failed to appear on the accustomed night. Isabelle never knew who he had been or what was the reason for his melancholy, and in moments of superstition she was half inclined to agree with Khadija.

Such solitary and mysterious experiences and the lonely wandering over the surrounding hills were the only moments that left an impression of reality. She was living on two levels, and sometimes it seemed to her that she was two separate beings. One of them was the sensualist, inexplicable to herself, animated by 'a strange desire to suffer, to drag my physical self down into dirt and deprivation'; the other was the contemplative, the awakening mystic, filled with the half-formulated desires for perfection and the still vague ambition to consecrate herself wholly to a great cause.

The European colonists, as well as most of the Arabs, were naturally unaware of this second side to her nature, and it was this period in her life that gained for Isabelle their lasting reprobation and a reputation for debauch which is still solidly linked to her name in North Africa.

She was as reckless with her money as with her health and her reputation. Soon the little sum left by Madame de Moerder began to run out. She who had spent without counting, both for herself and for others, now began to make economies which, since her whole attitude to money was quite unrealistic, generally ended by running her into added expense. The publication of *Yasmina* had roused her hopes of making a career in journalism, but they were soon frustrated. The literary level of the colonial press was heart-breakingly low and the few Tunisian journals showed no interest in her sketches of native life. The *Mektoub* seemed to be forcing her out of Africa, back to the drab, unhappy life in Geneva.

Early in the following year Isabelle returned to the Villa Neuve. Augustin, who had toyed with the idea of farming in Algeria, had failed to find suitable ground, or else had disliked the life or the hard work involved, and returned to Geneva at the same time as his sister. Both of them hoped to realize their mother's legacy—blocked in Russia and still non-existent for practical purposes—and return as soon as possible to their chosen lives.

They found Trophimovsky terribly aged. The old man lived alone in the big, rambling house, among the memories of the dead. The loss of his companion had left him inconsolable, and he was haunted by the tragic end of poor Vladimir. Even the garden interested him no longer and weeds were allowed to sprout unchecked in the treasured rockery, while the rare shrubs grew wild, untended and unpruned. He was suffering from cancer of the throat, was in almost constant pain and could sleep only with the aid of massive doses of chloral.

Isabelle was moved to pity for the old man. She who had been in constant revolt against her father, who had so often accused him of oppression and injustice, now began to remember his good points. Although the memory of her childhood had always been linked with suffering and 'Vava' had caused most of that suffering, she could realize now that his intentions had often been excellent and that he had been above all a victim of his own character.

She and Augustin did what they could and the noisy, awkward Isabelle proved, not for the last time, to be a surprisingly gentle nurse. An old friend often came to keep her company at the villa—Rehid Bey, 'Archivir', the 'brown-eyed Levantine' whom she had loved in her adolescence. He must have found her astonishingly changed after an absence which, after all, had lasted for less than three years. The sentimental girl who had dreamed of Istanbul, her heart torn between an absent brother and an indifferent lover, was a woman now, and one who could meet him on his own ground. Both were Moslems at present, but enlightened Moslems, each with a personal philosophy that owed little to the Koran. Archivir had enriched his natural intelligence by long contact with a group of Russian intellectuals and militant anarchists. He had a curious creed, or rather, a spiritual road by which he hoped to advance towards perfection and which consisted in the development of all his physical needs to their extreme limit and then turning all his available energy, moral and physical, to satisfying them. It was a doctrine of purification through the satisfaction of the senses which he had perhaps learned from the Dukhobors, the curious Russian sect, outlawed and persecuted in its native land, of which a number of members had taken refuge in hospitable Geneva.

Isabelle disapproved violently of this theory and believed that, in order to attain perfection, it was essential to reduce the needs of the body to a minimum and thus preserve the full sensitivity of the mind. On the other hand, they agreed on the necessity of heroism, on the grandiose mission of Islam in the world and the role which it reserved for the élite of its sons.

'How strange it is', wrote Isabelle, 'that all those singing words like Faith and Glory, on the lips of this intellectual, have never rung false in my ears. He is the only one of his kind in whom I have never found dissimulation, hypocrisy or lack of understanding.'

So there were long discussions during winter afternoons in the neglected shrubberies or beside the stagnant watercourse —discussions such as Isabelle had never known with anyone save Augustin, but which surpassed those talks on the Salève and on the Jura road, because of her new companion's intellectual superiority. She was explosive, tender, argumentative, sometimes behaving like a noisy schoolboy, then brusquely changing into a romantic yet already experienced woman. Her beauty, which was to fade so quickly, was in full flower and she was overflowing with mental and physical exuberance.

Archivir's old indifference was swept away. He began to speak of marriage and even wrote a formal letter to Trophimovsky, demanding Isabelle's hand. For her part Isabelle was undecided. She longed for stability, for she distrusted her own changing and uncertain character and feared the excesses into which it sometimes led her. She had often dreamed of a home and a companion on whom she might lean and rely, but on condition that she should be free to lead the life she had chosen, that the companion should not be a European—and above all not a Russian—and the home not in Europe. Archivir was one of the few Orientals who might have accepted her curious conditions. He could apply for a post in Tunis or Oran; beside him, Isabelle might have combined the advantages offered by East and West. Trophimovsky made no opposition and she even wrote to Eugène Letord announcing her engagement. Yet the marriage did not take place. Perhaps it was merely postponed, or perhaps Isabelle feared the bonds of matrimony even more than she desired them. Perhaps they simply talked so much that the whole affair began to appear unbearably complicated.

Then an event occurred which swept Archivir temporarily from her mind. On the morning of 15th May 1899 the old philosopher died, either from the unforgiving disease or from an overdose of chloral. Isabelle found him lying dead in his bed and was more distressed than she would have believed possible a few years earlier. Perhaps she mourned him less for himself than because he was the last link with the beloved dead mother. One by one all those whom she had loved were leaving her, 'returning to the original dust', as she noted sadly a few months later; solitude was closing in on her.

Trophimovsky was buried in the cemetery at Vernier, in the grave next to that in which Vladimir had lain for just over a year. His will was simple, for he had little to leave and disliked complications. The Villa Neuve was left to Isabelle (mentioned simply as 'daughter of Madame Nathalie de Moerder') and Augustin ('son of Madame Nathalie de Moerder and General Paul de Moerder'). There was no other bequest but there followed a curious condition. A copy of the will was to be sent to the Grand Duchess Elizaveta Feodorovna of Moscow, together with a statement of the value of the property, or alternatively, of the capital realized by its sale. This property was to pass to her or her descendants after the death of the two legatees and the proceeds to be used for charity in memory of their mother. A codicil, added shortly before his death, requested that the funeral should be as cheap as possible. 'For example,' suggested the ex-pope with characteristic realism, 'my body might be taken to the cemetery in a fourth-class hearse.'

No one could have been less avaricious or less interested in money for its own sake than Isabelle. If the legacy consoled her to some extent for her father's death, it was simply because the sale of the Villa Neuve would open the gates of Islam to her once more. It was the path to freedom, and Isabelle, without troubling to reckon the sum she was likely to get or stopping to reflect on possible difficulties, immediately began to plan how she would use it. So far she had touched only on the fringe of Africa, known only the semi-westernized town-dwellers. Now she would go out into the desert, penetrate that vast Sahara which had tempted her since she had first set foot in Algeria, cast off for ever the hated civilization of Europe—and attain fame at the same time as the chronicler of Arab life.

Augustin had his plans too, although they were less precise than those of his sister. The days when they had planned together miraculous journeys in the Orient were over for him. Like Isabelle, he desired above all to escape for ever from the sinister villa, from the ghost of Vladimir and the memory of his mother's sufferings and his own unhappy childhood. Apart from that, he found it difficult to make up his mind. The brief ambition of farming in Algeria was over—indeed, his experience in the Foreign Legion had finally disenchanted him with the East. Vaguely he planned to buy a house somewhere, to 'settle down'. Isabelle listened to him with a sort of despair, and perhaps repeated to herself, with a new bitterness, the cry of love and sorrow which she had sent out to him nearly four years earlier: 'Where are our make-believes, our hopes, our plans for the future?'

But in all this scheming, this mingling of mourning and hope, one person had been forgotten. This was Acobina, legal wife of Alexander Trophimovsky. The news of her husband's death soon reached her in Odessa, together with details of his last bequest. She immediately opposed the execution of the will in the name of herself and her children.

There could be no sale till the matter was settled. The Villa Neuve was sealed by the police, while lawyers argued and wrote endless and incomprehensible letters. There were papers to be signed, procedure to be decided on. Isabelle, disgusted and bored to death, thought only of escape. A sum of ready money—the proceeds of a mortgage or something of the sort —was immediately available. Anything seemed better than these long weeks of inactivity and legal havering. She signed a procuration, giving full power to Augustin to negotiate in her name, fled to Marseilles and took the first ship sailing for Tunis.

Lawyers and financial troubles were forgotten as soon as she landed once more on African soil. There was the lovely white town, hardly spoiled by the wide boulevards which the practical but unaesthetic French had cut through it in emulation of Baron Haussmann, stretching in tier after tier of gleaming white terraces down to the dark blue sea. There were the souks, a third almost of the whole town, where the light filtered sparsely through whitewashed arches, so that the thronged lanes were splashed with alternate sun and shadow, as if it were some strange world deep under the water. A single jujube tree guarded the entrance, then came a dark and almost silent passage, then suddenly the leather souk with its tumult of men, women, children and donkeys; then the meat souk, and the sweet-sellers, the souk of cotton and the souk of gold. There were the cafés where the great Negroes from the Sudan sprawled and chattered, others where dreaming Arabs listened to Berber pipers playing their monotonous, wailing tunes on the bagpipes; others which were love-markets, their clients encouraged by suggestive dancing and mimics.

Tunis, indeed, is still one of the most beautiful of African cities, although a few years before Isabelle first saw it, various improvements effected by the administration had rendered it more hygienic but less picturesque. Yet she was too impatient for departure to taste the joys which it had offered her at her earlier visit. She had hardly landed before she began to make plans for her journey across the desert.

Chapter Five

IT never occurred to Isabelle to make any special preparation for the journey. She merely packed a few necessaries and a couple of note-books in a bundle, furnished herself with some letters of introduction, and set off. The first stage of the journey was the interminable train journey to Batna, where she remained long enough to rewrite and give its final form to the story *Yasmina* which she had published in Bône. At the same time she took a step which was partly suggested for her own security but corresponded above all to her desire to escape from herself, to liberate herself from the past and identify herself wholly with Islam. Almost negligently, then, she shed both name and personality. Isabelle Eberhardt, the Russian amazon, no longer existed and in her place was born Si Mahmoud Essadi, a Tunisian student and man of letters. From this time on, Isabelle signed his name and generally adopted the masculine gender when writing of herself in the French language.

From Batna she rode to Timgad, then, skirting the fertile region of the Aurès mountains, came to well-watered Biskra in its verdant oasis. She was bound for El Oued, deep in the

Sahara. This region, inhabited mainly by nomad tribes, was still in the unsettled stage of colonization and was controlled by a purely military administration.[1] Eugène Letord, the correspondent of her girlhood days in Geneva, was stationed there and had promised his aid and protection. Although he had been one of the deciding factors in her departure from Europe, they had not yet managed to meet. He had intended to await her in Tunis but, just before her arrival, had been ordered to rejoin his regiment in the desert. No doubt he was as eager as herself for this long-delayed encounter. Isabelle's letters, with their contradictory statements, their romantic inventions, their illogical mixture of slangy cynicism and naïve idealism, were enough to rouse anyone's curiosity. That he was intrigued is certain; perhaps he was a little in love with his unknown and unpredictable correspondent. At any rate, he had already rendered her a number of services and probably hoped to reap a tardy reward.

There Isabelle discovered that the permission of the Arab Bureaux would be necessary if she wished to wander further south. The authorization was not easy to obtain. The officers of the Bureaux, detained by duty in a murderous climate, martyred by heat and malaria, could not understand why anyone should wish to travel in the Sahara at the height of summer for their own pleasure. Isabelle's costume—or disguise, as it seemed to them—increased their suspicions. She was interrogated sternly. A lieutenant-colonel inquired subtly whether she was a Methodist. Missionaries had been known to make uncomfortable and futile efforts to convert the tribes to various forms of Christianity and the French suspected these missionaries of being agents of the English, more interested in prospecting for possible political advantages for their country than

[1] By the year 1900, the coastal regions of Algeria had passed under civilian control with native representation, while the region south of and including the line formed by the towns of Tiarit, Saida, Bou Saada, Biskra, were administered by the military, each region being under the jurisdiction of an 'Arab Bureau'. In 1902 these regions became known as the Southern Territories.

in the spiritual welfare of the Bedouin. When Isabelle replied indignantly that she was a Russian and a Moslem, he became completely bewildered.

A certain Captain de Susbielle, who had been present at the interview, took a more conciliatory view and, managing to meet Isabelle at dinner that night, proposed that she join his convoy for Touggourt on the following day. Isabelle accepted, perhaps a little half-heartedly, an offer which would ensure safety and comfort but reduce the element of adventure. In the evening, however, she set out to explore the Old Quarter, with its fantastic Negro village and splendid, scintillating Jewesses. Here, in one of the cafés, she got into conversation with two young Arabs, named Saleh and Bou Saadi Chlely ben Amar, to whom she confided her projects and perhaps her identity. At the name of de Susbielle she noticed an immediate change in their manner. Pressed to explain themselves, they admitted, after many hesitations, that the captain was highly unpopular. He was one of those French officers whom Isabelle was to portray unmercifully in several of her stories—proud and disdainful, considering any mark of friendship or even of humanity shown to a native as a sign of weakness, upholding exclusively the interests of the French, even against the most legitimate claims of the inhabitants.

Isabelle did not stop to investigate the degree of truth in these stories. She had undertaken her journey in the hope of making discoveries about the customs and habits of the southern tribes and depended on them rather than on the French for the success of her undertaking. If she were to travel under the protection of a man to whom those tribes were hostile, she was assured of failure from the start. Before she left the café she had arranged to make the journey in the company of Saleh and Bou Saadi, and in the morning she greeted de Susbielle with some vague excuse. He set off without her, apparently convinced and suggesting a rendezvous *en route*; but rancour seems to have grown on him slowly, since he lost no opportunity in the future of doing her a disservice.

All day they loitered in the cafés, gossiping of the affairs of the South with some Spahis and the sons of one of the local marabouts. At two in the morning they set off, riding for Borj-Saada through intense heat. A caravan of Berbers of the Chaouiya tribe was resting by the route, where the three travellers joined them in a game of cards. Later, the old cheikh proposed that Isabelle should teach him French, but as they were due to separate within a couple of hours his progress can have been only slight.

They were out in the desert now, with its endless dunes, white or silver-grey according to the light, and gleaming with mineral salts. This was the moment for which it seemed to Isabelle that she had been waiting all her life. Here at last was complete freedom—freedom in space and freedom to live entirely at her own will. She was truly and completely a nomad now. She could ride like a mad thing, flying over the desert for as long as the fancy took her or as long as her sturdy little bastard-Arab horse could carry her, losing—in her own words—'all sense of reality in a sort of superb intoxication'. When she was tired, or when night fell, she was happy enough to roll herself in her burnous, take another burnous for a pillow and sleep in the shelter of some sandy ridge, banked up by the wind, or to doze in a ramshackle Moorish café among the palm trees of some tiny oasis. Attacks of fever left her weak and sometimes half-conscious, but could not diminish her joy; once she nearly perished in a dried-up salt lake; for several days no food was available and she lived uncomplainingly on dry bread and the water carried in true nomad style in the gourbi slung at her belt.

When the time came to take leave of her two companions, she started off alone, relying on chance companions, travelling now with a group of soldiers of the Foreign Legion, now with a Negro returning to his village to divorce his wife, now with a caravan from the Chaamba country, led by a courtly cheikh who refused all payment for his services. The company of these diverse wanderers deepened for her the intoxication of liberty because not one of them suspected the hated identity which she hoped to throw off for ever.

Her new rôle as Si Mahmoud afforded protection in the still uncertain lands of the South. It was a common thing for young Arabs of learning and good family to travel, sometimes for years at a time, before settling down to found a family and adopt some well-considered profession. As all study, in Islam, is related to the Koran and the teaching of Mohammed, these students held a place rather similar to that of the 'clerks' in Europe at the end of the mediaeval period. Their lives were secular but the mere fact of their learning gave them a semi-religious status. They would often cover immense distances to visit some holy man renowned for his piety or wisdom, remain for a time under his protection, then ride on again, just as the contemporaries of Villon would tramp from one distant university to another in order to sit under some re-nowned professor. They would ride on camel or horseback, sometimes singly, sometimes two or three together, depending if necessary on the rough hospitality of the Bedouin for food and shelter. These same Bedouin, some thirty years earlier, would not have hesitated to murder and rob any stranger—indeed, any man not belonging to their particular tribe—who was rash enough to travel otherwise than in a numerous and well-armed caravan. Since then, the French had roughly put a stop to this time-honoured habit and the desert was now comparatively safe.

The holy men who entertained these wandering seekers after truth and on whose hospitality Isabelle often relied were known as marabouts. Although the pure creed of Islam has no place for devotion to saints and admits no intermediary between man and God, maraboutism, the cult of holy men, had spread rapidly, especially in Morocco and Algeria since the sixteenth century. Most of them were descendants of the Prophet and thus supposed to possess the *baraka*, or divine spark, by right of birth. It was also possible to become a mara-bout through wisdom, good works, asceticism, mystical practices, while popular superstition lent a marabout quality to madness and even idiocy which, in these primitive regions, was regarded as a sort of divine folly sent by God. In general, only the hereditary marabout was recognized as such during his lifetime. Except in a few exceptional cases, those who acquired sainthood during their lifetime were venerated only after their death, although their descendants were marabouts in their own right until the *baraka* was allowed to fail by some neglectful or impious son.

The region through which Isabelle passed during the long journey from Biskra to Touggourt was rich in maraboutic tradition. It was impossible to go far without noticing one or more little domes rising out of the sand—*qoubbas* covering the remains of some saint. Certain tribes, such as the Ouled sidi-Chikhi that wandered in Southern Algeria, were entirely maraboutic, every man and woman a possessor of the *baraka*.[1] Stories were passed from mouth to mouth of the miraculous gifts of some of the most famous saints—there were modern saints like Sidi Bou-Sif, in the Oranais, who could name approaching visitors before they came into sight and tell the fortune of each; and Lella Fatma, the woman marabout who had been a prophet, foretelling future events with remarkable exactitude, while most of the great marabouts of the past had several miracles to their credit.

Dotted over the country were the domed *zaouias*, which were the homes of the marabouts and which served as temples, schools of Koranic science, courts of law, inns where travellers might live free for as long as they pleased, and inviolable sanctuaries for the pursued or the oppressed. Some of the celebrated marabouts who inhabited them, with the immense influence which they wielded over often considerable areas, caused a good deal of anxiety to the French, so that a European of uncertain sex, disguised as an Arab, and making use of their hospitality, would naturally arouse immediate suspicion.

The presence of the equivocal stranger was soon signalled to the Administration. When Isabelle arrived in Touggourt she found Captain de Susbielle in charge of the local Arab Bureau.

---

[1] Curiously enough, the Ouled-Nail tribe of Northern Algeria, famous for its customs of prostituting its daughters at adolescence until they are ready for marriage, is also a maraboutic tribe.

Their meeting was stormy, starting with a violent scene which gradually calmed to an icy politeness. The captain had been nursing his rancour and revenged himself for his disappointment by forbidding the Chaamba cheikh to guide her down to Wargla. It was only with the greatest difficulty that she obtained from him guides to take her directly through the Suf up to the oasis and administrative centre of El Oued.

When she arrived there at last, it was to find that Eugène Letord, on whom she had counted so much, had once more been abruptly transferred to another region. The officers, in spite of his recommendation, were openly suspicious and Captain Cauvet, in charge of the annex, had been scandalized when, informed that a lady wished to see him, he had encountered a slender young Arab whom he had taken for the servant of the lady in question, but who had turned out to be Isabelle in person. Later, at dinner, he had been impressed by the variety and vivacity of her conversation, but did not allow himself to be seduced by such frivolous considerations. He did not trouble to hide his conviction that she was undesirable. She was suffering, too, from attacks of fever that left her prostrated with weakness. Everything combined to force her out of the desert back to the enslaving life of civilization.

These few days during which she had seen the Souff, devoured by the sun, through a mist of fever, had been enough to decide her vocation. 'The first vision of El Oued', she wrote later, 'was for me the complete and definitive revelation of the harsh and splendid Souff, with its strange beauty and also its immense sadness.' From henceforth she was a nomad of the Souff, attached to that portion of the desert as if she was really one of these dark-skinned, aloof men of the Chaamba or Rebaia tribes, who passed on their delicately stepping camels, disdainful of the faithless Europeans whose way of life seemed to them so futile. When after many vicissitudes she found herself again in Africa, it was to the Souff that she returned, as if to her own home.

In the healthy region of the Aurès she recovered from the bewildering fever. There was a brief visit to Bône, a pilgrimage to the gay little cemetery where the 'White Spirit' reposed among all those others who had died in the faith of the Koran —an eternal exile in death as she had been in life. Here, too, there was the long-delayed encounter with Eugène, an encounter which, for once, was entirely satisfying and strengthened the ties of this strange friendship. A little later, indeed, Isabelle noted that Eugène was the only European to whom she had ever been seriously attracted.

It was hard to think of return. Riding from Bône through the olive groves of the Tunisian Sahel, Isabelle delayed from day to day, passing the autumn in glorious freedom, in mad gallops over the windy hills and night-long smoking of *kif* in the company of the gentle villagers of the coastal regions and the taciturn Bedouin who paused there on their lifelong journey. Thus the weeks passed and it was not until winter had set in that she reached the coast.

Chapter Six

WHEN Isabelle returned at last to Tunis she was penniless. Letters awaiting her brought nothing but disappointment. The affair of the Villa Neuve had made no progress whatever, and indeed, thieves had profited from its abandon to enter by night and steal most of the removable property. The inactive Augustin had given it up in disgust and gone back to Marseilles, leaving a procuration in the hands of a neighbour, a certain Monsieur Samuel. A letter written a little later informed his sister that he had married and begged her to visit him and make the acquaintance of his wife.

He was waiting for her when she disembarked and took her to his home. The flat was situated in a poor and depressing quarter of Marseilles. His wife was a simple young woman of working-class family who measured everything in life by the standards of the small bourgeoisie and by what she had been brought up to consider 'respectable'. She must have been horrified by this eccentric sister-in-law, with her cropped hair, her innumerable cigarettes and her affectation of the manners and language of the typical *voyou*. Isabelle probably showed herself at her worst. She would have disliked any wife chosen by Augustin and she realized at once that the influence of

PENCIL DRAWINGS BY ISABELLE EBERHARDT OF HER HOME IN
ALGIERS AND A DESERT SCENE

Photos kindly lent by M. R. L. Doyon

EL OUED, THE MARKET PLACE

Photo by Ofalag, Algiers

'Jenny the Work-girl', as she contemptuously called her, would inevitably break the slender thread that still bound him to herself. He had passed to the other side, joined the ranks of the conformists. The only being who had understood her as she wished to be understood seemed to her now like a shadow of the brother she had known.

*   *   *

It was already winter when Isabelle arrived in Geneva. The lake was a sheet of iron grey, the snow-covered mountains seemed to have drawn closer, looming up on every side around the little town. The hollow was bathed in fog and often the wind and the rain whirled down the Valley of the Rhône, lashing the lake to fury.

Isabelle hurried to Vernier. The two tombs, plain stone slabs unadorned by any Christian symbol, standing side by side near the tiny chapel on the brow of the hill overlooking the river, were already neglected, with the grass growing high around them. There was no one to bring flowers or to care whether the guardian tended them or not. Only the little school-mistress—she who had been called in by that terse note from Trophimovsky on the morning of the poor 'cactophile's' death—may perhaps have visited them. The ex-pope had no other friends in Vernier and his nihilist acquaintances would have considered any thought for the dusty relics of the body as false sentimentality.

The pillaged Villa was in an even worse plight. It had almost the aspect of a ruin in the midst of a wilderness. Isabelle, wandering miserably in the dripping garden, reflected that she alone, of all those who had inhabited that unlucky house, seemed to have escaped the course of destiny, to be free and to have life before her. She could truly describe herself as the only survivor, for Augustin had renounced the struggle and was already marked by the hereditary taint of neurasthenia which was to lead him, like his brother before him and his daughter after him, to take his own life.[1]

[1] Augustin committed suicide in Marseilles in 1914, and Hélène his daughter, pregnant and deserted by her lover, killed herself ten years later.

'Luckily', she wrote a month or so later, 'my whole life, all my adolescence, has gone to make me understand that tranquil happiness is not for me, that solitary in the world, I am destined for a relentless struggle against it; that I am, one might say, the scapegoat for all the iniquity and all the misfortunes that have precipitated to their fate those three: Mamma, Vladimir, Vava.'

It was a time of moral crisis, hard, but, as she recognized herself, essential for her development. She was living for the time being in a pension in the rue de l'Arquebuse, frequented by Russians. Here she renewed acquaintanceship with the *milieu* of anarchists whom she had frequented in her girlhood and she discovered a new friend, one who was to have an important though brief influence in her life. Vera Popova was a medical student and a passionate revolutionary who must have resembled in many ways the ardent Vera of Turgenev's famous novel—the first portrait of a nihilist in fiction—*Virgin Soil*. She was an intransigent intellectual, but Isabelle considered her as the most truly human person she had ever met. In her company she began to analyse herself more objectively than she had done hitherto, and above all, to question the rather childish romanticism by whose standard she had so often measured her own thoughts and acts. An extensive acquaintance with writers who happened to appeal to this side of her nature had passed with her for a wide culture. Under Vera's influence she was soon noting:

'I am becoming more and more ardently aware of the necessity of working tremendously hard at cultivating my intelligence. It is like a field that has been growing wild, almost untouched, and is much less developed than that of my soul.'

Vera encouraged her to believe that she had a vocation as a writer, forced her to work seriously. She was preparing sketches of the Sahel and had begun a novel, *Rakhil*, which she intended to be 'an advocacy of the Koran against the prejudices of modern Islam' and at the same time 'a song of eternal love . . . to intoxicate voluptuous hearts and those which are in love with art—which amounts to the same thing', but of which she was soon writing disgustedly that it now seemed to her 'a badly written collection of police dossiers'.

Isabelle was incapable of moderation in anything and, above all, in her human relationships. The friendship with Vera was profound and passionate. It was the first intellectual communion of her life—the first time, perhaps, that she had come in close contact with someone who was intellectually her superior, or rather, who had a better organized mind. Vera taught her to take stock of herself, to live according to her own nature, without feeling the need to explain or excuse herself.

'One must learn to *think*', she notes in her diary after one of these conversations. 'It is long and painful, but without that there can be no hope of individual happiness—that happiness which, for natures like my own, can only come from the existence of a *special world*, a closed world, which ought to permit us to live and be sufficient for us.'

Loving and admiring Vera as she did, it distressed her greatly that her friend should be divided from her in her opinion of two vital points—faith and love. Their discussions on these points were endless and were often shared with two other pensionnaires—a Bulgarian whom Isabelle called Chouchia, and another Russian known as Ga Hahn. The four of them passed their nights in arguments on literature, religion, philosophy. Isabelle flamed in defence of Islam and of that sublime love for which she had always longed, in spite of all poor Trophimovsky's lessons. Vera was disillusioned, cynical. She believed neither in one nor the other and was apt to despise those who looked outside themselves for consolation. Chouchia, who was in love with Isabelle and was trying to persuade her to return with him to his own country, naturally took her part, but Vera remained unshaken.

When Isabelle argued with her friend over faith and love she thought of Archivir, of their old, tormented love and the burning faith which he alone shared with her in this alien land. The young diplomat was stationed in Paris and came often to Geneva. The two saw each other frequently and sometimes they even still spoke of marriage, but both knew that their destiny did not lie that way. Occasionally there were outbreaks of the old violence, scenes, jealousy, despair, but nevertheless their passion was gradually cooling to a more fraternal love. Vera, to Isabelle's grief, refused to understand how dear to her were the memories of the old love and the resolution, which they took together, to replace it by an eternal friendship. Perhaps she was jealous for Chouchia, her compatriot, perhaps a little for herself, and she despised on principle the romantic nature of their attachment.

These friendships, this intellectual fermentation, took Isabelle's mind off the unhappy state of affairs at the Villa Neuve. Monsieur Samuel, to whom Isabelle and Augustin had tossed over the conduct of their affairs in a moment of boredom, was looking more and more like a villain. He was full of plausible explanations but had so far produced no results whatever, while the negotiations as carried out by him became surprisingly expensive. Augustin had taken himself off to Cagliari, counselling patience, and left her to cope with the muddle he had created. Presently he wrote that a child had been born —a little girl whom they had named Hélène. He described the wild, deserted landscape of Sardinia—landscapes which were reminiscent of Africa. It seemed that nothing could be done with Samuel; the lawyers seemed likely to squabble for months. Isabelle's desire to see the child overcame her repugnance for 'Jenny'. She decided to stay for a while in Cagliari and complete the manuscript which was to start her on a literary career.

★   ★   ★

In the tormented landscapes of Sardinia Isabelle took stock of her life. At the age of twenty-three she found herself totally alone—alone as are those very old men and women who have watched death pick off their family one by one till only they remain. 'The White Spirit', Vladimir, Vava, had returned to their original dust; Augustin had withdrawn into a world

68

where she could not follow him; Archivir belonged to a dream existence of peaceful happiness which would never be translated into reality. His image haunted her and often, perched on the great crags overlooking the sea, with Tunis invisible across the horizon, she asked herself how soon he would console himself with some other woman—one who would keep his house, be always close to him but who would never give him all that she would have been able to give if the 'Mektoub' had not forbidden it.

'I have renounced the hope of having a corner of my own in this world; a home, peace or fortune. I have put on the uniform—often very heavy to wear—of the vagabond and the *sans-patrie*. I have renounced the joy of returning to one's own home, finding one's loved ones there, and rest and security.'

Then again, reading over the collection of note-books in which she had recorded her life from day to day, she realized that:

'All the notes which I have taken so far might be summed up in these few and simple words: the incessantly repeated constatation of the bottomless sadness in my heart and in my life; allusions which became gradually vaguer and vaguer, not to people I have met or things I have observed but simply to the impression—invariably sad and dreary—that these people and things produce in me.

'Useless and funereal notes, miserably monotonous.

'The note of joy and even of hope is completely absent.'

The curious thing about all this is that there is never any question of rebellion, of trying to alter the fate for which she felt herself bound. Slav fatalism, Islamic resignation, or simply a profound knowledge of herself and a realization that certain trends of her nature were so strong that she *must* follow wherever they guided her?

Then, again, she would hear Archivir's words ringing in her head: 'Go on, Mahmoud! Accomplish great and splendid things. Be a hero!'

Then she would remember that she had vowed to consecrate her life to the glory of Islam. The memory of the summer in the Souff, the autumn spent in the Tunisian Sahel, would rise up with almost unbearable poignancy. The limitless stretches of sand, the burning desert wind, the call of the *muezzin* floating from some crumbling village of the Touggourt—to be out there again, free, delivered entirely to her own nomad instincts, seemed worth all the hardships and all the sacrifices. . . .

Her own experience and the practical counsel of Vera and Archivir had by now instilled a little common sense in her. She would return to the desert but with the backing of some editor, perhaps of the Geographical Society, at least with a literary reputation that would assure her an entry to the Press. Then she would have an influence, she would be listened to, she could uphold the cause of Islam more effectively than could a penniless and unknown wanderer.

The 'Journal' of the Goncourt brothers which had been her constant companion at Cagliari and of which she noted that it was 'a book which makes one think *deeply*', had given her an image of Parisian literary life that was stimulating though by now misleading. The French language was her chosen medium,[1] Paris the artistic capital of the world. A few months in Paris, she felt, would give her a firmer basis from which to take up her wandering life and put it to some account.

The Turkish editor, Abou Naddara, who had encouraged her youthful ambitions, was a prominent figure in the literary society of Paris, where orientalism was luckily in fashion. He would introduce her to the literary salons where she would meet other and more influential men of letters who might be interested in the project of a book describing the life of the Sahara. It may have been he who suggested that she address herself to Lydia Paschkoff, his close friend, her own compatriot and one of the most intrepid of female explorers.

[1] Isabelle's diaries, stories and fragments of novels are all in French. A few letters written in Russian show, I am told by those who know the language well, that she used her mother tongue somewhat inaccurately.

A letter addressed to Yalta in the Crimea, where the ageing amazon had retired from her wanderings in Egypt, brought an intriguing though mainly discouraging reply:

'I understand you,' wrote Madame Paschkoff in her first letter dated 18th March, 1900, 'and I understand your taste for the life of a traveller. It is the chase for dreams, and what do we do here but dream! I am speaking of intellectuals. But, alas, the body is heavy and cumbersome. You realize that, since you are coming to France (as I did myself from Egypt in 1889) to go in for journalism, which Abou Naddara and I know to be nothing but a life of vegetating and publicity. From time to time one's name appears in the papers and one is spoken of well or ill, and it matters not at all!

'In France one must be *French* to live from journalism and have—as I was told but refused to do—a lover in the Press. A husband is more difficult, but those who have a husband manage to make a career for themselves. . . . Never! I prefer to tell you all this brutally. I am told that even George Sand could have got nowhere without Sandeau, Musset, etc. Séverine got on because of her lovers Va . . . and Puy. . . . And they are Frenchwomen.

'My job on the *Figaro* was a miracle. I had the whole staff against me, except one, who was in love with me, and he let me down when he saw that there was no hope. All the Russians were against me, and when the Ambassador invited me to the Embassy it did me more harm than anything else. Jealous Russians have spoilt everything for me. Avoid the Russians. It is they who destroy their compatriots. They go about spreading lies, backbiting and degrading, and are not satisfied till they have done you immense harm. Russians are a pest, and above all those in Paris. Count Leontoff will tell you so. The Russians would not leave even him in peace in Africa.

'In my opinion you might make a name for yourself in Paris, but you will never make money. But, besides making a name, you might give some lectures by going to see the people for whom I will give you letters and whom I will ask to give

71

you others. I will tell you to whom you should address your-self directly and who might take a travel article; you might even find someone who would employ you to travel. Get in touch with the explorers: Prince Roland, Count Leontoff, Prince Henri d'Orleans. The first and last are immensely rich. So is the Prince of Monaco. Only it is necessary to find some way of introducing yourself so that you will not be taken for an adventuress. I will help you to do so.

'In spite of everything, the French are very domestic and like women who are above all good cooks. The woman writer seems to them a useless phenomenon. Show my letter to Abou Naddara. He will tell you that I am right and that I see clearly—too clearly.

'At present France is given over to internal quarrels; the Exhibition will bring a respite; after, it will all start again. And when France is given over to political parties, art and literature suffer. . . .

'Perhaps you will be lucky. My own luck lies in bringing success to all the people I introduce in Paris. . . . I will send you letters for Brieux, Aurélien Scholl, Madame Delphine Ugalde, M. de Santeuil, M. de Bois-Glavy, Bonvalet (the explorer), M. Georges Calmann-Levy. Bonvalet is a member of the Geographical Society and you have the right to belong to it. But you would have to pay 150 francs entry fee and 35 francs a year. In France one can get anywhere with money but nowhere without it. If you know Russian you can earn by writing in *Vremya*. . . . Wherever you go you should pre-sent yourself in elegant Oriental costume. Abou will tell you that his clothes did a lot to make him the fashion. I will also suggest to you the people to whom you should introduce yourself without letters.

'Write to me; how old are you?

'Avoid *La Libre Parole* like the pest. One must be friends with the Jews; they are intelligent people.

'Your devoted,
'LYDIA PASCHKOFF.'

Isabelle in Paris. . . . It is hard to imagine her, this shy girl who was at ease with the taciturn Bedouin and the rough Spahis and who loved nothing but the wild liberty of the desert, in the glittering salons of fashionable men-of-letters. It was early spring when she arrived—the lovely season when the avenues are powdered with gold from the sunlight drifting between the pale green leaves of lime trees and chestnut trees and a thousand spires shimmer in the soft new light. It was the year of the Great Exhibition—perhaps the most brilliant year that Paris has ever known. Tourists flocked from every part of the world; the streets were ablaze with light; the great *couturiers* clothed the beauties of the age in models of matchless elegance. The first underground line, running from Vincennes to the Porte Maillot, was opened with tremendous ceremony by President Loubet. Each night Edmond Rostand's two famous plays, *L'Aiglon* and *Cyrano de Bergerac*, drew unprecedented crowds; Sarah Bernhardt was at the height of her triumph; money flowed almost uncounted and prosperity seemed eternal.

Yet of all this novelty, all this brilliance, Isabelle made no note in her diary and seems, indeed, hardly to have noticed the events that were drawing the eyes of the world to Paris. During the whole stay the only comment she found to make was a brief reflection on the cemetery of Montparnasse, where she had wandered one night, seeking perhaps to evoke that other cemetery of Bab-el-Gorjani and the blind beggar in his grey rags who at its gates implored the Faithful for alms, in an unceasing litany, in the name of holy Bel-Hassein-Chadli:

'Reflected that all the great pulsation of Paris beating all around could not disturb the ineffable sleep of those who rested there.'

Yet she followed Madame Paschkoff's advice, conscientiously taking the necessary steps for breaking into the French Press. She called, for instance, on Séverine, the famous French feminist, who had launched Eugénie Buffet and many another young woman on a profitable career. She was editor of *La*

Fronde, the only journal that had dared to defend the anarchists, whose proclaimed policy of violence had made them the bogey of the French bourgeoisie. She had defended Ravachol, who had murdered in the name of anarchy and sung on his way to the guillotine:

> *Pour être heureux, nom de Dieu!*
> *Faut pendre les propriétaires!*
> *Pour être heureux, nom de Dieu!*
> *Faut couper les curés en deux!*

She had protested when Vaillant, another anarchist, had been condemned to death for throwing a bomb from the gallery of the Chamber of Deputies, although no one had been killed; she had proclaimed that the Lay State had 'shut up Heaven without opening the bakers' shops' and had reproduced the anarchist battle-song of which the chorus ran:

> *Mais pour tous les coquins*
> *Il y a de la dynamite!*

Isabelle, the contemplative, was far removed from such violence, but Séverine had been a heroine to the anarchist *milieu* in Geneva, a militant of the style admired by Vera. She had constantly defended the rights of women to a life of their own and a liberty equal to that accorded to men. The claims of the dispossessed *fellaheen* of North Africa could not fail to move her. Lydia Paschkoff had assured her that Séverine, if she wished, could open many doors to her.

Isabelle made the call obediently. She was too shy to follow her mentor's advice and wear the Arab costume which would make her conspicuous and immediately interesting, but she arrived at the offices of *La Fronde* dressed in her usual masculine clothes. The disillusion was rapid. Séverine, who was a notorious Lesbian, misunderstood Isabelle's appearance and the disillusion killed any interest she might have taken in her. The young Russian was not to take her place among the circle of protegées.

The old Turk, Abou Naddara, gave her a better reception

and she soon became a familiar of his salon, where she met Orientals, Islamists of various nations and a good number of more or less worthless hangers-on in search of the romanticism of the East without the trouble of going there. Abou Naddara had become, by one of those inexplicable caprices of the capital, a fashionable figure in Paris, but he had remained a Moslem of the old school, grave and kind, a little remote from the society of the Infidels who went into ecstasies over his picturesque dress and formal Oriental courtesy. He welcomed Isabelle as a co-religionist, gave her good advice and talked with her of Islam. It was the only house in Paris in which she felt a little at home.

A third salon, perhaps the most curious of all, to which Isabelle was invited through Lydia Paschkoff's recommendation, was that of 'La Ratazzi', widow of an Italian minister, born Marie Bonaparte-Wyse, and great-niece of Napoleon Bonaparte. A determined and vivacious old lady, she had been engaged, for political motives, to Napoleon III but had escaped the marriage and vowed a bitter hostility to her ex-suitor and the Second Empire in general. Although no one took her very seriously, she had managed to get herself expelled from Paris for writing a book attacking the Empress Eugénie. Under the Third Republic she had returned to the capital and installed herself in the Boulevard Poissonière, where she received anyone who cared to visit her, enthroned like a mummy in her vast salon, covered with jewels, swathed in lace and completely deaf. She was editor-in-chief of the *Nouvelle Revue Internationale*, and Isabelle was advised to visit her and to write for the review, although her mentor warned her that the old woman never paid her collaborators if she could help it, in spite of her great wealth.

Isabelle presented herself, armed with Lydia's letter and encouraged by the assurance that there was no need to dress up for the visit. The salon was frequented by an extraordinary and motley crowd, comprising men-of-letters, diplomats from Spain and South America, hungry artists, young women wearing smoking jackets and equivocally exquisite young men. Sometimes the famous poet, Catulle Mendes, appeared, his once cameo-like profile drowned in pasty fat, his shirt-front bearing the relics of many a good meal. He was a survivor of the epic struggle between the Parnassian and Symbolist schools that had shaken literary Paris during the *fin-de-siècle*, the friend of Anatole France, of Mallarmé, of Hérédia.

Isabelle, whose acquaintance with modern poetry went no further than Baudelaire, and whose taste was for Victor Hugo and Lamartine, gained little from such encounters. She made no impression and found few friends. In the unaccustomed dress of a European woman she felt clumsy and awkward, but she was too timid to draw attention to herself by appearing in burnous and turban, as Lydia had advised her to do. Paris was a failure; it had no place for her and left her with the firm conviction of her 'radical inaptitude for becoming part of any sort of group or feeling at ease among people who have been united by a passing hazard and not by a life in common'.

She had visited Paris only in order to make a name for herself in the French Press, and that she desired only as a means of fulfilling her dream of a nomad life in the desert. The enterprise looked like being a total failure, but the 'Mektoub' had its instruments everywhere, even in the salon of the Ratazzi.

She met her destiny there in the shape of the widow of Antoine de Vallambrosa, Marquis de Morès. The marquis had been a Spanish-Italian-French nobleman-financier who had married an immensely wealthy American, set up a series of business enterprises and distinguished himself in an epic struggle against a Jewish-owned beef trust. He had returned from the United States after amassing a prodigious number of dollars to enter the political life of France and consecrate himself to the Royalist Party.

The marquis had his own ideas about organizing the return to the throne of Henri of Orleans and the overthrow of the Republic. In his opinion that Republic had been founded by the rabble and was maintained by a conspiracy of the Jews. He became the chief lieutenant of Alfred Drumont, director of that review, *La Libre Parole*, against which Madame Paschkoff had warned Isabelle, and carried on the campaign of anti-semitism which the Dreyfus affair had set in train and which had shown no sign of dying out after the Esterhazy revelations and the revision of the judgement. As he was a noted duellist, he was able to play an active rôle by provoking those who disagreed with him. Indeed, he had only just avoided getting into serious trouble when he had called out and killed on the duelling field an unfortunate little Jewish officer who had had the temerity to stand up for himself and his race.

However, the marquis was more than a mere bully and had some original political ideas which his vast wealth allowed him to put into practice. He believed that the Royalist cause could not be won by the nobility alone but must be based on the support of the masses. He saw himself as the liaison between the aristocracy and the workers, got himself elected as deputy and organized in the proletarian quarter of La Villette a band of supporters, known as the 'Friends of Morès' and pledged to restore the throne of France. Soon he had three thousand butchers from the local slaughter-house rallied behind him, and each Sunday he would drive in his handsome *calèche* through those sordid streets with their odour of blood, while the butchers marched in his rear shouting 'Vive Morès! Vive le roi!'

It was natural that such a man should have many enemies and almost inevitable that he should die a violent death. Besides being a business man and a politician, Antoine de Vallambrosa was an explorer in his spare time. Like Count Leontoff, the Prince of Monaco, and so many powerful aristocrats of the day, he was drawn by the Sahara and the great North African colonies, with their endless possibilities. In 1896, while he was on an expedition in Southern Tunisia and Algeria, the marquis was assassinated in a region near the Tripolitanian frontier. His murderer was never discovered and, according to his widow, the Arab Bureau had no desire to throw light on the affair.

This was the story that the marquise told Isabelle in the

once-brilliant salon, now sadly degraded, of the old woman who had refused the title of Imperial Princess. Isabelle knew the region, spoke of villages where Morès was known to have passed, cited the local tribes. Her one desire, she confided, was to return to the desert, but the Paris venture had failed, she had earned no money and little reputation and no longer had the means to pay even a passage to Tunis. Madame de Morès immediately recognized the possibilities in Mahmoud Essadi. In next to no time it had been arranged that she should finance an expedition to the region and that Isabelle should attempt to solve this four-year-old mystery.

Chapter Seven

I seems that, now that the return to Africa was at last possible, Isabelle hesitated before taking a step which she guessed would be final. In spite of all she had suffered in Geneva, in spite of the morbid depression which overcame her each time she revisited the scene of her childhood, the town drew her like an inescapable magnet. There were the memories of the disappointed love for Augustin; memories of the dead, those whom she had loved more than she had admitted to herself in the old days of thwarted revolt; there was Archivir—

'the most charming of all those whom I have met on my route and whose dear images remain with me, and his charm is the most noble, the finest that can exist: he speaks to the soul and not to the senses, he exalts that which is great and reduces all that is low and vile. No one has been able like him to understand and nourish those blessed things that have begun to germinate in me, slowly but surely, since the death of the "White Spirit" '—

there were Vera, the intellectual mentor, and Chouchia—'simple, good Chouchia'—who was beginning to act more and more powerfully on her affections.

So Isabelle came again to Geneva, plunged again into the atmosphere of intense intellectual speculation and passionate comradeship which was that of the pension in the rue de l'Arquebuse. There was the manuscript of *Trimardeur* to finish, notes to be made for the travel book which she planned to write on her journey to Ouargla—the desert village which the angry de Susbielle had prevented her from visiting the previous summer and near which the marquis had met his death. She was to start from Algiers, but Algiers was 'too well known', so that Bône was to be the starting place in the book. The strange landscape of the marshy Oued 'Rir would provide 'a few beautiful, melancholic pages in the nature of African silhouettes,'[1] and she would follow the same track to Touggourt. There were other interesting perspectives in view. The terrible Berber Sheik, Bou-Amama and the Rogni—rival to the Sultan—were carrying out a constant, harrying guerrilla warfare on the Moroccan frontier supported by their fanatical peoples. According to the trilateral treaty this frontier, although its delimitations were of the vaguest, must not be crossed by the French troops nor must any permanent posts be established in the vicinity. Now, public opinion in France, roused at last by news of the senseless massacre of border troops, was demanding action against Bou-Amama. There was question of a punitive expedition, troop movements to the South, the establishment of a formal and well-fortified frontier. Isabelle realized at once the opportunities this would give her. She had not renounced her hopes of making a brilliant career as a journalist. The Moroccan expedition, if it came off, would provide a unique opportunity for anyone familiar, like herself, with the language and customs of the natives:

'If, this autumn, there is a march to Morocco, I shall follow, of course, taking careful notes.'

If, during these weeks of friendship and literary planning,

[1] Luckily Isabelle's style was brief, colourful and devoid of artifice. She never wrote as badly as she intended to write and the purple passages which she used to plan out were never achieved.

SI LACHMI BEN BRAHIM, CHEIKH OF THE QADRYA OF EL OUED

By courtesy of the Musee Franchet-d'Espercy, Algiers

ISABELLE EBERHARDT DURING HER LAST VISIT
TO ALGIERS, AGED 27

Madame de Morès' money slipped rapidly through her fingers and looked like being seriously diminished before she ever set foot in Africa, it was of little importance. There was the Villa Neuve, Trophimovsky's legacy, awaiting the clearing-up of a few final points by the solicitors.

Gradually, though, it appeared even to the unsuspecting Isabelle that something was wrong in the affair of the Villa Neuve. M. Samuel was invisible. He neither replied to letters nor could be found at his home. The lawyers were vague. They had advanced sums in the name of Isabelle and Augustin for the judicial proceedings and the upkeep of the villa, but, in M. Samuel's continued absence, it was difficult to explain just how these sums had been used. Certainly the villa itself, which was looking more dilapidated than ever, did not seem to have benefited.

When it became clear that there was nothing she could do and that the little money she had would barely suffice to carry her to Ouargla, Isabelle realized that she must leave Geneva. It was strange for her to have to drag herself away, almost unwillingly, from this town which had for so long been like a prison to her. Now, though, the separation was almost too brutal, too final. She was about to bid a last farewell to all the links with her past and to the few human beings whom she still loved, and go out into a loneliness almost unbearable for a girl of twenty-three. Even before the visit to Paris, when she was already in sight of this final leave-taking, she had written in her diary:

'And now I am a nomad, with no other homeland than Islam, with no family and no one in whom to confide; alone, for ever alone in the proud and darkly sweet solitude of my own heart; and thus I shall continue my way through life until the time comes for the great, eternal sleep of the grave.'

Now the time had come to translate these words into reality. On 21st July, 1900, Isabelle sailed for Algiers on the boat *Eugène-Pereire*, after making some haphazard arrangement that the money she still hoped to receive from the sale of the

Villa Neuve should be forwarded there to Eugène Letord.

The stay in Algiers was short. It was marked by a happy and peaceful day spent with the faithful friend and adviser, Eugène, in the bare little room he had rented for her; by the purchase of a little pipe and a supply of *kif*, to the smoking of which she had returned with pleasure but which had not yet become a necessity; and by a moment of intense religious fervour—the first, perhaps, in which she had the intuition of an Islam other than the picturesque or heroic aspects which had acted purely on her imagination.

On the evening after her arrival she had gone in the evening to the mosque of Djemaa Djedid for the *icha*, or evening prayer, and on her return recorded the experience in her diary:

'Entered into the cool dusk, hardly lighted by a few oil lamps. Impression of old Islam, mysterious and calm.

'A long wait near the *mihrab*. Then, from far off, behind us, there rose up a clear, high, fresh voice, like a voice in a dream, making the responses to the old Imam standing in the *mihrab* and reciting the *tatiha* in his quavering voice. Then, standing in line, we prayed, between that alternation of two voices, at once intoxicating and solemn; the one in front of us, broken, old, but little by little swelling, becoming strong and powerful; and the other, streaming as if from above, out of the depths of the dark mosque, at regular intervals, like a song of triumph and unshakable faith, radiant . . . announcing the coming victory, the inevitable victory of God and his Prophet. . . . Felt an almost ecstatic feeling swelling in my breast in a flight towards the heavenly regions from which the second voice seemed to come . . . with a note of melancholy happiness, serene, gentle and undoubting.

'O, to be lying now on the carpet of some silent mosque, far from the stupid noise of the corrupt city, and listen, to infinity, with closed eyes and with the eyes of the soul lifted to heaven, to that song of the triumph of Islam.'

It is not easy to decide whether Isabelle's outbreaks of religious fervour were the result of a truly mystical *élan* or the reactions of an artist to the rites, grandiose in their austerity, of Islam. Above all, perhaps, as she hinted in a passage of her diary already quoted, Islam stood for her as a sort of symbol of the homeland and family of which she was deprived in their reality. She had been a rebel from the real home, the real family, but Islam offered the possibility of escape into a heroic, colourful and yet contemplative world in which she might make her home and develop a personality for which there was no place in Christianity and the civilization of the West. From now on, at any rate, she was to give herself entirely to Islam, penetrate some of its most recondite mysteries and become, in the eyes of many of the tribes of Algeria and Tunisia, a sort of saint.

It was in this state of peaceful identification with the life of her adopted land that Isabelle set out on her journey to the South. This time she was in haste and there was none of the delicious loitering on the way; the carefree, wild gallops far from the comparatively safe track that had made her first expedition so strange and enchanting an adventure.

From Algiers she travelled by train, mingling unconcernedly in the crowded third-class carriage with the motley collection of Arabs of the poorest sort and Negroes from the distant Sudan or come up from the interior. All were ragged, many were verminous, but they murmured the five ritual prayers through the interminable day, their heads bowed roughly in the direction of Mecca. They were her brothers in Islam, and among them she felt happy and at ease. At her side travelled Mokhtar, a very young Arab with whom she had spent the last day in Algiers and whose company helped her to enjoy the tedious journey—first over the wild Kabyle mountains, then over the high plateau beyond the Iron Gates, then across the desolate plain around Bordj-bou-Areridj.

From Meroier Isabelle rode by mule through the desolate and lovely Oued 'Rir, with its invading odour of saltpetre; then at Biskra she hired a horse and pushed on through Our-lana, sleeping at Sidi Amram on the ground, beside a fire of dried dung, under a sky in which the stars were so bright and innumerable that the earth was bathed in brilliant light. As she advanced farther and farther into the desert she recognized once more the extraordinary permeability to exterior impressions which it seemed to lend her, and the serene, half-melancholy happiness which was for her the only real peace. At El-Merayer and Touggourt she paused to write her journal, noting the stages on the route and the diverse aspects of the country through which she had passed; then, between two such notes, her happiness seemed to break out in a sudden cry;

'O, Sahara, menacing Sahara, hiding your beautiful dark heart behind your inhospitable and dreary solitude!'

On the 31st July she was in Touggourt, soliciting a permit for El-Oued. It was granted and two days later, accompanied by the guide Habib, she rode through Ferdjane, across the dunes, where she noted the strewn dead bodies of several camels. Then they entered the little town, alive with soldiers and black-turbaned nomads.

'Alighted in front of Habib's house, in the middle of the street. Reflected on the strangeness of my life.'

The first visit to El Oued had been an almost mystic revelation and the town enchanted her anew, as it had done the previous year. Built on the slope of a high sand-dune, with its principal houses plastered to glistering whiteness and its winding unpaved streets, it was purely Arab, its aspect at least untouched by the Europeans. There were the two markets, with their arches and cupolas, one for meat and one for grain, to which men of all the tribes of the Souff came thronging, on foot or riding on asses or camels, crowding the roads on Thursday evenings to be ready for the Friday sales. She had seen the wild men of the Chaamba there, and black Soudanese, and the mysterious blue-veiled Tuaregs who occasionally rode up on their *meharis* from the untamed South.

The military headquarters, the barracks, prison, hospital, were white as the native buildings. The mosque was near the centre and the *muezzin*'s tower rose high above the squat domes of the town, bathed in the blinding desert sun.

Isabelle was in high spirits, careless of whatever difficulties might lie before her. Her health, she noted with pleasure, was excellent, apart from an occasional access of light fever—the toll of the desert. The house of a local *caïd* was conveniently to let; she rented it and commenced to settle in, although her luggage had not yet arrived and she had only her camp bed and a few cooking utensils. Her note-books were piled on the floor and she was only waiting till her installation should be a little less provisional before setting to work on her numerous projects. As for money . . . there was none left. The *caïd* was not yet paid, nor was Habib. Each day's food and coffee was a problem. She was expecting a sum to be sent by Eugène from Algiers—probably from the Villa Neuve. Until it came there would be debts, the sale or pawning of the small poor objects she owned, a whole series of nagging worries that prevented concentration on literary matters. Apart from that, there was the pleasant, almost hypnotized laziness induced by the heat and the monotony of the endless white dunes, stretching on every side as far as the eye could see; there were the intoxicating rides, far from the beaten tracks, the tiny oases, the night camps and the coffee drunk early in the morning, before re-saddling, at the moment when the desert stretches like a sort of diaphanous grey muslin.

'I must remember', she reminded herself in her diary a few days after her arrival, 'that I did not come to the desert to give myself up to the *dolce far niente* of last year, but in order to work; that this journey may turn out to be the sinister shipwreck of my whole future, or else the road to salvation, material as well as moral. This will depend on whether I can make my way or not.'

Then this good Moslem added a note in Arabic—half pious resignation, half touching of wood:

'Everything is in that which has been written.'

One may wonder what, meanwhile, was becoming of the affairs of the Marquise de Morès, who had financed the expedition and was expecting to wreak vengeance, through her agent, on her husband's murderers. Yet there is no further mention of the matter in the diaries and Isabelle seems to have settled in El Oued with the idea of remaining there for the rest of her life and writing books on the life and customs of the Sahara. There is no more question of going to Ouargla and the permit was probably refused once more in Touggourt, since there is a brief note that, after all, her health would have been far more menaced in the stifling region of the far South than in El Oued.

From that time on, the whole matter seems to have slipped from her memory, yet rumour travels fast in the desert and it was not long before the officers of the Arab Bureau were instructed as to the original motive of her journey. She herself had probably forgotten all about this motive; but it caused grave displeasure in military circles and the officer in command of the Annex of El Oued—who was later to be mingled in another manner with her destiny—wrote after her death, in answer to an inquiry:

'I knew Isabelle Eberhardt only very slightly, and indeed, my functions obliged me to maintain a certain reserve towards this person when she arrived in the Souff. . . . I congratulated myself on this reserve when, later on, I learned that she had come in the pay of Madame de Morès in order to investigate the death of her husband, which had given rise to all sorts of inquiries with which I was charged myself. I can only say that the first impression she produced on me was detestable, but I was obliged to recognize later on that this woman, who was highly intelligent, was quite inoffensive from the French point of view.'

Isabelle was thus obliged, from the beginning, to suffer the hostility of the Europeans among whom she dwelt. It touched her little. She had experienced it at her first visit and later, during the rest of her life indeed, it was to complicate and darken her existence. Now, though, in the joy of exploring the Sahara, they hardly existed for her. They were the infidels, excluded from the great Family, unreal figures, puffed up with their importance, unbelievably insolent to the Arabs and happily unconscious of the disdain in which these held them. The people of the desert—her people—were Habib, with his immense family, his brothers, his old father and his mother:

'. . . with a whole mountain in her head; plaits of black hair, plaits and tassels of red wool, heavy iron rings in the ears, held up by strings hooked in the head-dress. When she goes out she throws a blue veil over all this. A strange, bronzed figure, ageless, skinny, with lifeless black eyes. . . .'

Abd-el-Kader ben Taleb Said and Mohammed el-Hechni, both cunning, secret men; little Misbah and his father, the Deira of the *Caïdate*, who lent her his ill-favoured little white horse for her expeditions into the surrounding territory; and the *bach-adel*, the usurer who pressed her so warmly to accept a loan (but Trophimovsky's daughter, who had been trained to check every article delivered to the house and never to trust the tradesmen, suspected that he was not as disinterested as he seemed and resolved to avoid his services if it was humanly possible).

Some of these Arabs were cultivated men who held all learning in high esteem, and Isabelle's literary projects—or rather, those of their companion Mahmoud Essadi—interested them highly:

'Take care, Si Mahmoud', said one of them to her one day when she expressed the pleasure she took in her new existence. 'You will become used to our life and you will always put off your work from day to day. Then, in the end, to-morrow will never come. It is nothing but cowardice, a stifling of the remorse that comes from the protesting vocation.'

So Isabelle made notes, kept her diary scrupulously, began a manuscript in faulty Russian entitled 'Life in the Sahara'. The heat was abating, the fever left her and she was able to work a little, at the price of a good deal of effort and the sacrifice of hours which might have been spent, far from intruding humanity, on the Deira's horse, out among the dunes.

It was a bad horse, slow and heavy-mouthed. One day—Eugène must have sent funds from Algiers, although they could not have proceeded from the Villa Neuve—she bought a little Arab horse of her own, named him Souff, and explored the surrounding country with even greater joy and at a much better speed. Souff remained her companion for the rest of her stay there and they were deeply devoted to each other. He would follow her about the town like a dog, to the astonishment of Europeans and natives, eat beside her when she ate and sleep close to her at night. On him she accomplished the deeds of prowess that gained her the reputation of one of the best riders in the desert, forced the admiration of the French and earned her more sympathy from the Arabs than ever her learning could do.

It was Souff who carried her one evening to the garden of Bir R'arby which lay in a deep valley where, after the narrow entry, a steep and gradually widening slope swept down to a well, surrounded by high palm trees and cultivated plots bearing canteloupe and water-melons and fragrant sweet basil.

When she had wound up the dripping water-skin from the depth of the well, Isabelle drank deeply, delighted to find that the water was almost cold. Then she lay down to rest, rolled in her burnous at the well-side.

During the night in this garden Isabelle made the acquaintance of an Arab named Sliman Ehnni, a quartermaster of the Spahis. He was tall and slender, with a fine pair of moustaches and a liquid, melancholy gaze which had retained something childlike and innocent. He spoke good French and had a little instruction and a taste for the easier romantics.

It was far from being Isabelle's first caprice, but Sliman's ardour was so intense and satisfying that it provided her with what was practically a new experience. From the beginning, the charming Arab began to make plans for eternal love.

Isabelle, touched but sceptical, reflected rather sadly that her own heart had aged, that there were too many memories of other, disillusioning experiences, for her to be able to believe, like her partner, in the indefinite duration of love. When Sliman made plans for the future, spoke of what they would be doing seven years from now, she could only smile and beg him to be content with the present. Sliman could not understand her, the mere idea of separation brought tears to his eyes, and Isabelle wept with him and reflected that experience can only be acquired by suffering and can never be communicated to others. It certainly did not occur to her that a year later she would re-read the diaries where she had first spoken of Sliman and make notes in the margin:

'Predestined garden! . . .

'Now a year has gone by and my life is more intimately than ever connected with his own.'

Meanwhile the present was sufficient for her. Sliman's days were occupied by his regimental duties but their nights were their own, and they spent them in long rides over the dunes and in visits to the many fertile little gardens—all similar to the delicious oasis of Bir R'arby—which surrounded the wells of the Souff.

Soon Sliman was frequenting the little white house rented from the *Caïd*. The liaison was becoming public and was commented on, without indulgence, in the officers' mess. The latent hostility of the Europeans which had been temporarily calmed by the quiet, withdrawn life led by Isabelle, burst out again. Some of it at least was rooted in disappointment. Isabelle had few claims to beauty, with her high, protruding cheek-bones, upturned Kalmuk-like nose and extreme pallor, nor had she a trace of what is usually considered feminine charm. She herself, with perhaps exaggerated modesty, set down the attentions of some of the younger officers entirely to the account of novelty and the dearth of European women. For this reason, or for that of her youth, her singularity and unusually beautiful and melancholy eyes, several Frenchmen had done their best to win her favour and were probably less affected by their own disappointment than at seeing a half-educated Arab preferred to themselves.

From the beginning, and on account of the Morès affair, Isabelle had been surrounded by spies, every movement reported by zealous agents to headquarters. Capitaine Cauvet, duly informed, had been obliged to recognize that her solitary expeditions into the desert were not undertaken in order to incite the tribesmen to revolt. As no one in El Oued could conceive that she might ride for days and nights together through the desert for the mere pleasure, the rumour that she was a sort of were-wolf, scouring the desert in search of prey, was soon creating a pleasurable diversion in the monotonous life of the garrison. Sliman's continual presence kept the gossip in circulation. Isabelle's financial affairs were also known to be more and more deplorable, for Madame de Morès had been informed by some means—perhaps indirectly through the Arab Bureau—that Isabelle was not showing much zeal for her mission and the subsidies from Paris had suddenly been cut off. The extreme poverty and austerity of her life, instead of disarming suspicion, caused her to be blamed for letting down the prestige of the European community—to which it never occurred to her to consider that she belonged. It was to be Isabelle's fate to be considered, wherever she passed, as a spy or an hysteric, simply because—as her later friend and confident Robert Randau, had pointed out—the average man, and specially perhaps the average colonial, cannot conceive that any course of conduct may have a motive which is purely poetic.

While the whispering and the evil suspicions grew around her, her poverty became really acute. She supported it stoically, having no one in whom to confide, pawned her few belongings and consoled herself for lack of food in the gentle stupor of *kif* smoking.

She was living, in fact, in a sort of strange dream of happiness. This rebel who flouted every convention of womanhood remained at the bottom of her heart a sentimental young girl, with the common longing for domestic bliss simply transposed into an unusual and uncomfortable setting.

'As for Sliman', she noted in her diary, 'nothing is changed except that I am becoming more and more attached to him and he is becoming truly a member of my family, or rather *my family* in himself. . . . May it last like this for ever, even here, among these unchangeable grey sands!'

And a little later:

'Yesterday I had yet another proof of the candour, the goodness and the beauty of Sliman's heart, which belongs to me. . . . In spite of all I have suffered and all I shall have to suffer, I bless God and destiny for having brought me to this unforgettable city in the sand to give me to this being who is my *only consolation*, my sole joy in this world where I am the most disinherited of all the disinherited and where I feel myself richest of all, since I possess this inestimable treasure.'

And the nomad began, like any of those bourgeois wives whom she had so despised, to make plans for the future—plans based, as ever, on the mythical revenue from the Villa Neuve. She and Sliman would buy a café in one of the neighbouring oases; Sliman's brother should run it, while they two would set up a plantation of vegetables not usually cultivated in the Souff, and at the same time a native grocer's store and a French café in El Oued itself. She would procure a fleet of camels and organize her own convoy for the transport of her goods. . . . The dream was precise, worked out in detail and gloriously impossible.

Sliman agreed to everything, lost in admiration of his companion. Isabelle had undertaken to complete his instruction, introduced him to her favourite authors, and especially to Loti, worked at perfecting him in the French language. He followed her directions with docility and wrote her charming love-letters during their periods of enforced separation. He seems to have been entirely subjugated by her. He was a man of uncertain health and dim personality who made no impression at all on those who knew the couple at that time and later. The prestige of a European mistress perhaps had something to do with the facility with which he seemed to have accepted a relationship so unusual in Islam, but his attachment was certainly sincere. He made up in intuition what he lacked in intelligence, and Isabelle imagined at least that he was the only person who had ever understood her. He was the Beloved, the new Augustin. Her heart, she noted, was at peace for the first time in her life, although her spirit was as unquiet as ever. In spite of material sufferings, she lived in terror of being obliged to leave El Oued, and it was almost a relief for her to reflect that she no longer had the means to remove even if she would.

'Here I am at last, in the state of utter destitution which I have foreseen for some time. And yet, in bringing me to El Oued, providence seems to have meant to save me from a destruction that would have been inevitable anywhere else.

'Who knows—perhaps these strokes of adversity will simply serve to change my character, to awake me from that sort of indifference to the future which often comes over me.

'Please God that it be so! Until now I have always come safe and sound out of the worst and most dangerous situations. Perhaps my luck will not desert me now. The ways of God are impenetrable.'

Chapter Eight

I SABELLE had arrived at El Oued at a moment when the French were having more than usual trouble with certain turbulent elements among the tribes. Their efforts to colonize and pacify North Africa had stumbled constantly against the factor of an alien and exclusive religion. From the purely political aspect, the Arab chiefs would generally have admitted that the domination of the French was gentler and more profitable than that of Turkey. Where the Turks had uninterested themselves completely from this unfruitful corner of their domain, the French built railways, cultivated the land (for their own profit, it is true), built hospitals and put a stop to the banditry which had held the Sahara in terror for untold generations. From the logical European point of view, the change was all for the better.

Such considerations, however, had little weight with the fanatical people of the Koran. The utter corruption of the Ottoman Empire and its representatives counted not at all against the fact that it was an Islamic power and the Sultan a Moslem, ruling from afar over other Moslems. The French, on the other hand, were a few hundred thousand infidels—barbarians in the eyes of every true believer—invading a holy territory and ruling by force over millions of the Faithful.

This hostility, based on religious fanaticism, had been the motive power of Abd-el-Kader's desperate resistance until his defeat in 1844, and of the continual insurrections in the Kabyle country until 1871. Now the country was officially pacified. The Arabs were inclined to resignation ('Allah has permitted the French to triumph', they said, 'therefore it is His will that the aliens rule for a time over us, since all strength is an emanation of His force'), though they were convinced that the final victory would be that of the Prophet.

The Arab Bureaux were well aware that the relative calm that reigned in the Sahara in this year 1900 was extremely precarious. The flame of revolt might break out at any one of a thousand points. Sometimes it would take the shape of isolated action and a French officer would fall assassinated at the hands of some semi-madman, inspired by the tongues of angels or by the local cheikh. These assassinations were becoming more and more frequent, and the inevitable connivance of the murderer's whole tribe made it hard to establish responsibilities. More occasionally there were insurrections—spontaneous or organized, for the roots of such affairs were inevitably tangled and confused. The revolt at Timmimoun was occupying the local Arab Bureau at this moment and having repercussions in Paris, where some awkward questions were being asked in the Chamber of Deputies.

The outbreak at Timmimoun, like all those which kept the Sahara and the Aurès in constant effervescence, could be traced, at least indirectly, to the influence of the religious confraternities. It was on them that peace or war largely depended, since they had absolute power over vast numbers of fanatic adherents and remained in constant contact with Mecca, with the Moslems of India and, indeed, with the farthest corners of Islam, so that unpredictable factors, often political rather than religious, might at any time intervene in their secret network, stirring unsuspected until deceitful peace erupted in violence.

These confraternities had been formed originally, at the

time when Islam was first menaced by the growth of the Shiite and Wahabite schisms, by austere and holy men known as the *fokra*[1] who wandered over the Arab lands seeking to restore the people to the primitive and venerable doctrine of Mohammed. Each based his claim to perfect orthodoxy on the teaching of some famous theologian and on that of all the wise men from whom those theologians had drawn their own wisdom, thus forming a sort of chain of pious links which, in order to render their teaching valid and indisputable, must stretch back without a break to the Prophet himself.

Gradually the followers of these holy men had formed themselves into chapters or confraternities, all based on the same principles and teaching, but each with its special character and practising certain prayers and rites which distinguished it from the others; the Klelonatya, for instance, practised isolation and retreat; the Qadrya were philanthropic and humanitarian; the Aissaouya specialized in the working up of mystical ecstacy. The Tidjanya were the only purely Algerian fraternity, without ramifications in the East, and were thus considered as allies of the French; while the most fanatical as well as the largest of the confraternities in North Africa was the Rahmanya.[2]

The organization of these bodies was extremely rigorous and their hierarchy rigid. Each confraternity had its Grand Cheikh, some venerated marabout who would wield immense power over a vast territory and numerous subjects. Under him was a *naib*, to whom he delegated part of his own authority; then came the *moqaddem*, or local cheikhs, who were also marabouts, reigning each over his *zaouia*, aided by a *reqab* or *naqib*, who would act as a sort of curate. Then came the mass of *khouans*, or initiates, sworn to absolute obedience to their cheikh, to secrecy in everything that concerned their order and to complete solidarity with their fellow-members.

The *khouans* might be students who lived in the *zaouia* and

[1] El fokra—poverty.
[2] In 1910, ten years after Isabelle came to the Souff, statistics estimated that 295,189 people were affiliated to the confraternities in Algeria alone.

would later go out as doctors or teachers among the tribes, where they would act as powerful instruments of propaganda for their confraternity; or they might be poor, unlettered Bedouins, who could neither read nor write and came to listen, half-understanding, to the words of the living saint. It mattered little, for there was a place for everyone in the organization and its teaching was supple enough to be adapted to the requirements and limitations of each. It would proscribe, according to the judgement of the cheikh, the use of amulets and superstitious practices to the primitive Berbers who were still hardly enfranchised from the old magic and fetish worship; it would initiate the learned into the secrets of religious ecstasy and philosophic speculations; while to the humble and weak it offered the more immediate advantages of the support of a powerful organization.

The esoteric nature of the confraternities made it difficult for the French, not only to penetrate them or obtain any influence in them, but even to know what was going on. Each *khouan* would only be able to reveal such things as were known to the mass of ordinary members and not the inner secrets of the organization. They thus remained the principal problem, and one which needed extremely delicate handling, of the colonization of North Africa. Every great cheikh disposed, in fact, of an occult army which he could manœuvre at his will, since each *khouan* had undertaken to be a passive slave in the hands of his cheikh and sworn to carry out any order, even if it involved his own death, without questioning or even seeking to understand.

The French had been forced to accept one defeat at their hands, when they had attempted to put a stop to the system of taxation which the cheikhs imposed on every one of their subjects according to his estimated means. On the other hand, a well-developed sense of practical advantages had induced many of these cheikhs to reconsider their general attitude and arrive at a compromise which allowed them to live on more or less friendly terms with their conquerors. Certain of the cheikhs had been useful allies, especially in the Aurès, where one of them had been largely responsible for crushing the Kabyle rebellion of 1879. Yet their allegiance could never be counted on and the French would have been in an even more delicate position if the different confraternities had not maintained violent feuds among themselves, much of their pugnacity being diverted to slandering each other, with occasional riots and murders to be revenged and counter-revenged, so that the French could maintain a certain advantage by playing the cheikhs off one against the other.

The power of the confraternities was especially great in the yet barely tamed South, and Isabelle had naturally come into contact, as a Moslem, with various *khouans* of El Oued and the surrounding oases. The confraternity of the Qadrya was especially powerful in this region, and her personality interested some of its principal members, notably Sidi Hussein ben Brahim, *moqaddem* of the *zaouia* of Guémar and one of the many sons of the great cheikh and venerated marabout, Sidi Brahim, who had recently died. Isabelle visited Sidi Hussein at his *zaouia*, talked with him and impressed him with her knowledge of the Koran. He believed her to be a Moslem by birth, since she maintained her story of a fictitious Russian-Moslem father. Perhaps he recognized her as a genuine mystic and believed that he could lead her along the way of Truth to the ultimate state of perfect unity with God—that is, saturate her with that Desire which is the only form that the love of God can conceivably take in Islam and which transforms the life of the mystic into a limitless ascension towards the Inaccessible. Perhaps he foresaw that this European, whom he believed to have the ear of the French, might be useful to him. At any rate, he must have believed in the sincerity of her conviction, for he welcomed her with simplicity into the order, even sparing her the usual period of novitiate.

There was nothing very unusual in the admission of a woman into the ranks of a confraternity, since female members were even allowed to attain the rank of *moqaddem* and give the initiation to other aspirants.

Isabelle received her initiation in the *zaouia* in the presence of a good number of local members of the Order. The ceremony was simple and almost homely. First the *moqaddem* shaved the neophyte's head and heard her recite an act of contrition and the vow taken by members. Then he placed a coronet on her head, a cloak over her shoulders, bound her with a girdle to the fellow-member she had chosen as a sort of godfather, and initiated her into the wisdom of the Order, explaining the meaning of *Sufism*, or the system of holiness recommended to members, which is neither a philosophic system, nor even confined to any one religious sect—since there have been Christian and Jewish Sufis—but which consists in living in a state of perfect purity, attained through sentiment and intuition rather than any special practice or intellectual process.

Then she received the chaplet of the Order and learned the semi-secret *dikr*, or short ejaculatory prayer which the most pious *khouans* recited almost continually during their waking hours and which served, with the chaplet, to make them known to each other and to evoke the obligatory aid and support of a fellow-member in the hour of need.

The *dikr* of the Qadrya consisted in the recital one hundred and sixty-five times at the end of each of the five ritual prayers of the day, the formula 'There is no God but God', and it was recited in a special style, prescribed by the holy Cheikh Snoussi and common to his sect and to part of the Qadrya. The *khouan* would sit cross-legged, touch the tip of his right foot and then trace with his hand the principal artery running round the intestines. Then he would place his open hand, with spread fingers, on his knee, while pronouncing the name of God in a deep voice, prolonging the final syllable as long as his breath held out. He was to pray not only for himself but for all those whom God had created in the same image and should continue 'until the heart and spirit attain the sweetness of ecstasy and receive the revelation of divine light'.

After this first part of the ceremony, the guests sat down on the carpet, while the *moqaddem* prepared sweetmeats which he distributed, sending some out to those members who were not able to be present. Then Isabelle recited the prayer of engagement:

'I seek near God a refuge from His anger and pray Him to restrain me from ever casting off the girdle, breaking the pact or disavowing the confraternity established by God. For whoever preserves the girdle, the pact and the confraternity, shall be preserved by God and obtain His blessing, but whoever shall cast them off will anger God and on the day of resurrection he shall show a blackened face, so that the angels shall curse him.'

Then, with her 'companion of the carpet', there was the exchange of question and answer through a long catechism; then she received the final diploma of the *khouan*. She was now a full member of a vast family that stretched to the farthest confines of Islam, every member of which was pledged to help her if she made herself known to him.

The Qadrya had been founded in the twelfth century by a teacher of Baghdad named Sidi Abd-el-Kader Djilani, whose teaching, like that of all the great preachers of the time, had aimed at union with God and the restoration of moral purity, and was based entirely on the Koran and the *Sunna*, or collection of the traditional sayings of Mahommed, but had developed through the centuries its own particular system for training its initiates and its distinctive character and practices. It professed, notably, a special reverence for Sidi Aissa (Jesus), and was not notably hostile to the French. Yet the father of their terrible old enemy Abd-el-Kader had been Grand Cheikh of all the Qadrya and his son's long revolt had been made possible by the support of the confraternity. On the other hand, it had played an important part in Algeria by helping to pacify the half-savage and semi-Moslem Berbers. On the whole it was on good terms with the authorities, but as the most popular and most powerful organization in the region, there was a tendency for all sorts of political adventurers to seek its support, and the Arab Bureaux at Touggourt and El Oued regarded it with a certain reserve, while its principal rival, the confraternity of the Tidjanya, was known to be unreservedly pro-French. It was among the Tidjanya that the French chose guides to take them to the hostile land of the Tuaregs; it was they who were chosen as interpreters and sent as agents to persuade unpacified tribes that their interests would be served by an alliance with the authorities. The Qadrya bitterly resented the favours shown to their rivals and the consequent jealousy gave rise to ceaseless intrigues, in which Isabelle was to play an important, though unconscious, rôle.

The support of the Qadrya gave her confidence and, in a way, conferred on her a sort of official standing in the desert. She was known to be the familiar and favourite of Sidi El-Hussein, and soon of Sidi Lachmi, whom she occasionally served in the capacity of secretary. The frequentation of such holy persons conferred on her a sort of mysterious prestige. She could ride without fear towards the South, live for weeks on end the life of the wandering shepherds, who received her as a tribeswoman for the love of Sidi el-Djilani, offered her the milk of their own camels and often made a corner for her in the tents where humans and animals slept, sharing their warmth, sheltered from the biting desert wind. In return she wrote letters for them when they were obliged to have recourse for some reason to a local cheikh or the French authorities, and helped them in sickness with a few simple medicines or counsels which they generally neglected in favour of the traditional prayers and charms.

Once, at least, her affiliation saved her in an unpleasant situation. It was towards the end of the autumn, a short while only after the initiation at Guémar. Isabelle had ridden out into one of the most abandoned regions of the desert, to the south of Taibeth-Guebla, on the route to Ouargla. She was camping, as usual, accompanied by her little servant Ali, among the shepherds of the Rebaia tribe, studying their customs, helping them with their troop of goats and hunting hares among the strange, almost nightmare vegetation that springs up in the Sahara at the moment of the November rains.

One night a violent sandstorm had torn up the Bedouin tent of black goat's hair under which she lodged. Tired, with nerves on edge, she had left Ali to repair the damage and ridden out on 'Souff' far into the trackless distance. Gradually, as the storm gathered again in the sky, she realized that she had lost her bearings. She rode to the west, to the south, and still there was no sign of the camp:

'Little by little the sky became covered with cloud again and the wind began to fall. If it had not been for the night's storm which had dried up and blown about the whole of the superficial layer of sand, such a slight wind could have caused no movement in the surface of the ground. But the earth was reduced now to the state of almost impalpable dust and the sand continued to flow gently over the steep sides of the dunes. Soon I noticed that my tracks disappeared rapidly.'

At last Isabelle discovered a narrow valley containing a small well, where she was able to drink and to water Souff, and where she prepared to spend the night:

'I was drawing up the water by means of a bottle attached to my belt when I heard a voice saying close behind me:

' "What do you do here?"

'I turned round: in front of me stood three men, deeply bronzed, almost black, dressed in rags, carrying their meagre baggage in canvas sacks and armed with long-barrelled guns.

' "I am thirsty."

' "You are lost?"

' "I am camping not far from here, with the Rebaia, shepherds of the Souff."

' "You are a Moslem?"

' "Yes, thanks be to God."

'He who had spoken was an elderly man. He put out his hand and touched my chaplet.

' "You belong to Sidi Abd-el-Kader Djilani. . . . So we are brothers. . . . We too are of the Qadrya."

' "Thanks be to God," I said.'[1]

[1] *Dans l'ombre chaude de l'Islam.*

Isabelle spent the night in listening to the strange story of the lives of these nomads and at dawn they brought her again to the camp of the Rebaia.

Although Isabelle's initiation into the Qadrya gave her such possibilities of a nomad existence and familiarity with the desert tribes as no other European woman has ever had, it did not increase her popularity with the French. Capitaine Cauvet, though a conventional soldier who had no patience with eccentricity, had been honest enough to consider Isabelle's case objectively and came to the conclusion that she was neither spy nor agitator, but not all his collaborators were so free of prejudice. Among the Arabs, members of rival confraternities saw with no favourable eye this inexplicable foreigner who was beginning to attain so strong an influence in the region. They asked themselves just what she was doing, why she had been accepted by Sidi el-Hussein; whether, even, she was truly a Moslem. She who wished only to live in retirement, to savour the delicious intimacy with Sliman and to work at her stories of the Sahara, was discussed in all South Constantine, watched, reported on and credited with far-fetched motives for actions whose basis was purely lyric.

Isabelle was at least half-aware of the whispering and the hatred. As the months went by, her existence became more and more solitary. Sliman lived with her now in the one-roomed house rented to her by a sergeant of the Spahis and to which she had now removed:

'We are in the Jewish quarter,' she wrote to Augustin, 'and in the neighbourhood of an old quarter, all in ruins, with abandoned houses crumbling to pieces, the proprietors dead or gone away to the desert. Among these ruins, which come to an end behind the white mosque on the market-place, one sees only a few clandestine Sufi prostitutes, vague shadows without fixed abode who come at night to hang around the Jewish taverns. I have definitely engaged a servant—a *kif*-smoker who is the personification of calmness and honesty.'

The room was lined with plaster—a sign of wealth in this

town where most of the houses were built of naked clay, with the sand of the desert as their only flooring—and it contained Isabelle's tin trunks, a rickety table, an iron chair and a bur mattress with a tent-canvas for covering. On the wall there were photographs of her parents, of Vladimir, of little Hélène, together with spurs, an embroidered bridle, her own revolver and Sliman's, a red burnous, a sabre and a rifle. From the room one could climb to a terrace, where she and Sliman slept during the hot weather and there was a courtyard in which Souff ate, slept and lived as one of the family. Apart from the schoolmaster, Abd-el-Kader, her servant and occasional long visits from Cheikh el-Hussein, she received no one. Sliman sufficed her and, when the money ran out and they were obliged to dispense with a servant and move to humbler quarters, she was glad to have broken off relations with the officers and Europeans.

It was at about this time that one of Si Hussein's brothers, Si Lachmi, returned from a journey to Paris which he had made in company with a third brother who held the important position of Naib and was known as a faithful friend of the French.[1] Isabelle had met Si Lachmi at Touggourt, at the time of her first visit to El Oued, and had been deeply impressed by his splendid appearance, his tall stature, flowing beard and the green robes which he wore constantly as a sign of his holy office. He was an astonishing horseman and could enthrall any audience with his conversation, so it was natural that the impressionable Isabelle should have fallen immediately under his spell. This spell, indeed, was so strong that Si Lachmi had managed to get himself accepted by a great number of the Qadrya as Grand Master of the Order, in spite of the fact that his father had not chosen him as his successor and that several of his brothers and an important faction of the confraternity refused even to consider him as a marabout, since his piety never went beyond words and his reputation for double-dealing and the scandals in which he had been involved made

[1] The Naib was to die at the battle of Timmimoun, a few weeks later, while attempting to play the rôle of mediator.

it impossible to take him seriously as a spiritual leader. Isabelle knew nothing of these internal intrigues, or else dismissed them with her usual disdain. She had never been a judge of character and a romantic physique or a golden tongue would always be enough to turn her head.

Si Lachmi's arrival was to be celebrated by a splendid fantasia in which Isabelle, who was as dare-devil a rider as any *Chaambi* or *Rebaia*, could not resist taking part.

The men of the Qadrya had come to a place near Ormes, some ten miles from El Oued, to meet the marabout, and she had passed the night with them, listening to the inspired discourse of the marabout. Then, at dawn, she had joined the great throng which waited, among the cries of servants, the impatient neighing of horses and the wild melodies of four Negro musicians come up from the land of the Nefzaoua, for the appearance of Sidi Lachmi.

'Suddenly from the crowd an immense cry rose up:
' "Hail, son of the Prophet!"
'The clamour continued, frenetic, and the tambourines, waved high above the heads, beat a mad cadence. The horses backed away at first in terror, then bucked, foaming, and hurled themselves forward.

'Impassive, mounted on a white stallion from the Djerid, eyes lowered and in silence, the marabout seemed entirely occupied in controlling his maddened mount.

'At last a sort of procession formed, white and sinuous, dominated by the great height of the green-clad marabout. We advanced slowly towards the East, as if to meet the rising sun which was still hidden behind the enormous dunes that ring El Oued. These silent, sterile dunes seemed to be giving birth to great masses of people. Whole tribes came riding over the hills, sprang up from the gardens.

'At last a great circle was formed and into it, singing a wild, irregular song—an ancient hymn of war—rode twelve young men, clad in brilliant Tunisian silks and armed with long, encrusted blunderbusses. They charged on us, simulating an attack, and discharged their arms all together and close up to our terrified horses, into the smoking sand. . . . The bitter, intoxicating smell of the burnt powder maddened men and horses even more than the savage music of the war-cries.

'Soon, over the crest of a high dune, appeared a white procession which seemed to come in a golden halo from the eastern light. Preceded by three ancient banners, green, yellow, and red, embroidered with faded inscriptions and surmounted by balls of gleaming copper, with tambourines waving above the turbaned heads, this crowd advanced, enormous and compact. There were neither cries nor the usual music, simply the muted counterpoint of the tambourines accompanying the single, overwhelming chant, breaking from thousands of breasts:

' "Hail and peace to thee, O Prophet of God! Hail and peace to thee, holiest among God's creatures! Hail to thee, Djilani, Prince of Saints, Master of Baghdad, whose name shines from the East to the West!"

' And the man towards whom all the love and confidence of this vast crowd mounted up, continued to walk slowly, silently, impassive and isolated among the noise and the acclamations.'[1]

The mad ride over the sands among this vast band of horsemen, back to El Oued thronged with the faithful awaiting the entrance of the marabout, left Isabelle in a state of extraordinary exaltation and roused her from the torpor into which she had been slowly sinking among the greyness and desolation of the desert in winter. It was bitterly cold and she had no fire and little food, but she roused herself, forced herself to write, abstained from *kif* and made good resolutions. Augustin had written, giving his blessing to her union with Sliman, which he had opposed at first, and she felt a great joy at this reunion from afar with her brother. At the same time she was enjoying a growing intimacy with Si Lachmi, acting as his secretary, listening to his advice and assisting at his councils. Her state of

---

[1] *Dans l'ombre chaude de l'Islam.*

mind was happy enough to make her forget—which she did easily enough at any time—that she was living from day to day, without resources of any kind.

This pleasant state of affairs did not last long. The 'Mektoub' had written that Isabelle was never to be left in peace or un-menaced. One day, shortly after the long fast of Ramadan, a terrible blow fell. Sliman was ordered away to Batna, far to the North and separated by the whole of the Souff and the Aurès from El Oued.

There was barely enough money to buy a few frugal meals for the following days and there was nothing left to sell which anyone would want to buy. It was useless to think of the expense of the removal, the journey and the re-installation at Batna. There were debts at El Oued which must be paid before departure. A separation should logically have been inevitable, and it was perhaps a desire to separate the couple and put an end to a local scandal that had been the motive for Sliman's transfer. The terrible night was spent in a vain seeking for forgetfulness in *anisette* and the stupor-bringing *kif*. As soon as morning dawned, Isabelle set off for the *zaouia* of Sidi Lachmi to implore the aid and protection of her cheikh.

She found the marabout sitting in his flowing green robes and white veils, among a horde of pilgrims who had come for his blessing and advice before setting off for one of the holy cities. It was impossible to speak; Isabelle could only draw him aside an instant to beg for a private interview in the evening.

She found Sliman haggard, feverish with anxiety and could do nothing to calm him before he left to take up his daily duty with his regiment. They were to meet again, at the hour of the magh'reb, by a cemetery on the road to the *zaouia*, but it was nightfall before Sliman appeared and his state of anxiety was so terrible that Isabelle feared at every moment to see him fall from his horse. When they were at last seated on the great red carpet, in the audience room where the light of a single candle left the corners in shadowy darkness and the cheikh waited gravely to hear their request, neither of them had the strength to speak:

'I saw that Rouh'[1] was weeping, and I, too, was ready to cry. But the Cheikh reminded us that all could come to him, that we must not betray one another.

'It took me a long time, in the state I was in, to explain what had happened to us and in what a situation we found ourselves. He remained silent, weighed down with care, as if absent.

'At last the Cheikh and I exchanged a glance in which I did my best to put my whole heart, pointing to Rouh', who was beginning to lose consciousness altogether, burning with fever. . . . Then the Cheikh rose and went into his house. . . .

'He came back a moment after and laid before Rouh' 170 francs, saying: "God will pay the rest."'

The worst was over, immediate debts were paid, but there were other expenses to be met before she could follow Sliman to Batna. Isabelle, who had never asked for help when she was cold or hungry, was ready to throw herself on anyone's mercy, to beg unashamedly, rather than be separated from her beloved Sliman. Sidi-el-Hussein and Si Lachmi had given alms, and now she thought of the third brother, Sidi Eliman, a blond, blue-eyed giant of a man, who was an esteemed marabout in a region a little to the East. Ali, sent to announce her visit, brought back the news that Sidi Eliman had just left with a number of *khouan* for Nefta, just over the Tunisian border, where a memorial service was to be celebrated at his father's tomb. Si Lachmi was about to make the same journey and Isabelle, who knew how to make herself useful to him, easily persuaded him to accept her in his suite. Her plan was to accompany him to Behima, a village some fifteen miles east of El Oued, where he was to meet his brother. There she would present her request to Si Eliman and return, if possible, on the same day to pass with Sliman the short time that remained to them before his departure.

---

[1] Beloved, darling.

Chapter Nine

I T was at Behima that there befell the strange and tragic adventure that transformed Isabelle from an obscure nomad to the principal actor in a *cause célèbre* that made her name notorious throughout the French North African colonies. The real motives of the participants, the shadowy figures who pulled the strings in the background, remain obscure in spite of all the speculation and inquiries that were made at the time. Even Isabelle's own explanation, based on her intimate knowledge of the ways of the confraternities, was incomplete and unsatisfying.

She had ridden to Behima on 27th January 1901, with Sidi Lachmi, a number of his *khouan* and her own servant, who was to accompany her on foot during the return journey, after the cheikh's departure for Nefta. The full story of the events of that afternoon is contained in a letter which she wrote from Marseilles to *La Dépêche Algérienne* on 4th June:

'We entered into the house of a certain Si Brahim ben Larbi and, while the marabout retired to another room for the afternoon prayer, I remained in a large room which led into an anti-chamber opening on to the village square where a compact crowd was waiting and where my servant was tending my horse. There were five or six Arab notables of the village or its surroundings, nearly all of them *khouans* of the Rahmanya.[1]

'I was seated between two of these persons, the owner of the house and a young merchant of Guémar named Ahmed ben Belkacem. The latter had begged me to translate three commercial telegrams, one of which, very badly expressed, was giving me some difficulty. My head was lowered and my burnous drawn over my turban, so that I could not see what was happening in front of me. Suddenly I received a violent blow on the head, followed by two others on the left arm. I raised my head and saw an individual—poorly dressed and thus a stranger among us—who was waving over me a weapon which I took to be a cudgel. I rose suddenly and rushed to the opposite wall to seize Si Lachmi's sabre, but the first blow had struck the crown of my head and almost stunned me, so that I fell on a coffer, experiencing a violent pain in my left arm.

'The assassin, who had been disarmed by a young *moqaddem* of the Qadrya, Si Mahommed ben Bou-Bekr, and one of Si Lachmi's servants, named Said, managed to break away from them. Seeing him approach, I rose and tried again to reach a weapon, but my giddiness and the acute pain in my arm prevented me. The man then rushed out into the crowd, crying: "I shall fetch a gun to finish him off."

'Said then brought me a blood-stained Arab sabre of iron and said: "It is with this that the dog wounded you!"

'The marabout, who had run out at the noise and to whom the murderer had immediately been named by several people who had recognized him, sent for the independent cheikh of Behima, who belonged, like the murderer, to the confraternity of the Tidjanya, who are, as everyone knows, the most irreconcilable enemies of the Qadrya in the desert.

'This singular functionary opposed an obstinate resistance to the marabout, insisting that the assassin was a cherif,[2] etc.

[1] The powerful and fanatical confraternity of the Rahmanya was on friendly terms with the Qadrya.
[2] Descendant of the Prophet.

'The marabout then publicly threatened to denounce him to the Arab Bureau and insisted energetically that the assassin be arrested and taken away. The cheikh gave in much against his will.

'The assassin was then brought into the room and laid on a mattress. He began by simulating madness then, convicted of lying by his fellow-villagers, who knew him to be in possession of all his wits and a quiet, sober man, he began to say that it was God who had sent him to kill me.

'As I was fully conscious, I was able to note that the man's face was quite unknown to me and I began to question him myself. He told me that I also was unknown to him, that he had never seen me before, but that he had come to kill me and that, if he was freed, he would make another attempt.

'When I asked him what he held against me, he replied:

' "I hold nothing against you, you have done nothing to me and I do not know you, but I must kill you."

'The marabout asked him if he knew that I was a Moslem and he replied in the affirmative. His father declared that he belonged to the Tidjanya.

'The marabout forced the local cheikh to inform the Arab Bureau and ask for an officer to take away the murderer and open an inquiry, and for the regimental doctor for myself.

'The officer charged with the inquiry and the doctor arrived towards eleven o'clock.

'The doctor found that the wounds on my head and left wrist were insignificant. A lucky chance had saved my life; a clothes-line happened to be strung just above my head and had intercepted the first blow, which must otherwise inevitably have killed me. On the other hand, the joint on the exterior of my left elbow was split open, the muscle and the bone damaged.

'I was in such a state of weakness following the enormous loss of blood which had continued for six hours, that I had to be left for that night at Behima.

'The next day I was taken on a stretcher to the military hospital of El Oued. . . .'

The name of the aggressor was Abdallah ben Mohammed, a man of Behima, well considered by his neighbours. When he was interrogated, first by the marabout, then by Captain Cauvet,[1] he simply reiterated: 'God wished it; God still wishes it.' Nothing else could be got out of him and he was removed to El-Oued to await his trial.

Meanwhile Isabelle was installed in the operating theatre of the hospital, while the doctor dressed and stitched the wound, aided by the young corporals attached to his service. Afterwards she was transferred to the little room where she was to pass nearly six weeks of pain and fever. There was a high, narrow bed, surmounted by a shelf bearing a jug of *tisane*, a tin mug, a spittoon: a table with a candlestick, tobacco, *kif*, and an accumulation of the little cups of coffee, which she had not the strength to drink. On the wall opposite the bed was

[1] Commandant Cauvet, whom the author was able to question in Algiers, affirmed his personal belief that the attack on Isabelle had been inspired by Si Lachmi himself in order to compromise the Tidjanya. Commandant Cauvet had retained, at the age of ninety, a clear recollection of the Marabout, whom he considered as an unmitigated scoundrel and double-dealer. The Bachagha of El-Oued, who knew both Isabelle and Si Lachmi well, gave her the same explanation, with additional details:

'Si Lachmi knew that Mademoiselle Eberhardt, whom we knew as Si Mahmoud, had come to El-Oued to discover the assassin of the marquis de Morès and he supposed that she had the support of the French. He believed that, through her, he could make the Bureau believe that the murderer was a Tidjanyi and that the crime was covered by the whole confraternity. After a time, he began to realize that Si Mahmoud had no influence with the French, who, on the contrary, had done all they could to prevent her interfering in the affaire Morès, and who had arranged to discredit her with the marquise. When he understood this, Si Lachmi wished to be rid of Si Mahmoud, all the more so because she was his mistress and he was beginning to tire of her. The attempted murder at Behima was organized by him to this end. We all knew that Abdallah was not a Tidjanyi but on the contrary a member of the Qadrya and that he was acting on the orders of his cheikh. Si Lachmi's intention was to make the French believe that the crime was the work of his rivals.'

The Bachagha added that Si Hussein was so disgusted by the unscrupulousness of his brother, that he left the region rather than remain near him. Isabelle, however, never doubted Si Lachmi's good faith.

a notice, written in the careful handwriting of some conscientious sergeant: 'Sanitary Service Regulations', terminating by a paragraph on 'Disciplinary punishments inflicted on civilian patients'. Outside the sentinel tramped ceaselessly up and down, from time to time there came the sound of brusque military commands, the knocking of a gun, the hoarse whispering of Arab guards.

In her weakness and incessant pain—for the cut muscle caused horrible cramps, with sudden, agonizing retractions of the hand or fingers—Isabelle became a prey to reasonless fears. She was afraid of dying—not of death itself, but of dying alone, without the comforting presence of any loved one. And indeed, she thought through the long nights of insomnia, there was no one left to her. Her whole family was dead except far away Augustin, upon whom she could no longer count, and she had been brutally separated from Sliman. She felt herself surrounded by hostility. Sometimes she was seized with terror at the idea that Abdallah might go unpunished. That would be a tacit permission to any of the Tidjanya to kill her without fear of reprisal and her life would not be safe for a day. Her anxiety increased as she realized that the incident was being, voluntarily or accidentally, stifled. The Algerian Press, usually ready to make the most of any Arab aggression, made no mention of the affair which should normally have provided a front-page sensation. Sometimes she even believed that her aggressor had been an agent of the French, paid to get rid of her. Then she would imagine herself, stretched out dead on the table of the autopsy room, just across the court-yard and clearly visible from her own window.

Gradually, a certain consolation came to her through the friendship of her doctor. Dr. Taste, when she had met him occasionally among the other officers of the garrison, had appeared to her cold and unfriendly, but now he revealed himself as kind and understanding. He himself was lonely out there in the desert, among colleagues for whom he had little sympathy, and gradually he got into the habit of confiding in Isabelle. He would pay her long visits, sit beside her bed and tell her, in his deep, bass voice, with its sing-song Norman accent, the story of his life, naïvely happy to find a listener, then, in his turn, calm her fears and reassure her so that she felt for him 'the gratitude I feel for all those who do not cast the stone at me, stupidly or insolently, and who guess what I really am and what I might have become if I was not so alone and had not suffered so much.'

One afternoon, when the early desert spring was beginning to bear its sun and heavy scents into the dreary hospital wards, Isabelle was watching the courtyard from her window when she saw two blue-clad *turcos* searching a prisoner. It was her aggressor, Abdallah, who was being transferred to the cells.

The sight moved her profoundly and that night she noted in her diary that it had caused in her, 'the strangest and deepest impression of *mystery* I ever felt'.

'However much I search my heart, I can find no hatred for this man, and still less contempt.

'The feeling I have towards this being is extraordinary: when I think of him, it seems to me that I am at the edge of an abyss, a mystery of which the last word . . . or rather, the last word of which has not yet been said and will enclose the whole meaning of my life. Until I know the answer to this riddle—and shall I ever know it; God only knows!—I shall understand neither what I am, nor what are the reasons and the goal of my destiny, which is one of the most astonishing that have been.

'Yet it seems to me that I cannot be destined to disappear without having become conscious of all the profound mystery which has surrounded my life, from its strange beginnings till this day.

'The incredulous, who adore ready-made solutions and are impatient of all mystery, will say "Madness".

'No, for the realization of what abysses are contained in life —abysses of which three-quarters of humanity know nothing and of which they do not even suspect the existence—can only be considered as madness from the same point of view as that of a man, blind from birth, who hears an artist describe the splendours of a sunset or a starry night.

'It is easy to tranquillize a timid soul, terrified by the proximity of the Unknown, by commonplace explanations, drawn from false experience, or by "generally accepted ideas" consisting of scraps of inconsequent thought, of superficial knowledge and hypotheses taken for realities by the immeasurable moral cowardice of mankind.'

Later, she even came to feel a sort of gratitude for this unfortunate man, an unreasoning fanatic and no doubt a mere puppet in other, more unscrupulous hands, who had brought her face to face with certain problems concerning death and her own relationship to God and the unknown, which she had, until that time, perceived only dimly:

'Evil', she noted again, after that pitiful glimpse of Abdallah, 'is a *disorder* in the functioning of God's laws and thus it is impossible for it to function in a regular manner. That is why, in all evil plans, there are so many torn links and so many pitfalls. By its very essence, evil must end badly for him who is its instrument.'

It was indeed on this evening, and dating from the moment of that glimpse of the unfortunate Abdallah, that Isabelle's vaguely mystical tendencies began to crystallize into a more precise form. Abdallah appeared to her at this moment as a martyr—even a voluntary martyr—who had submitted to being an instrument sent by God to open up a certain road to his victim, and that at the price of a lifetime of suffering for himself.

Isabelle, indeed, had never been content to accept the strange course of her life as the effect of chance. For a time, she had looked to her own nature as the source of her destiny. Trophimovsky may have sown the seeds of determinism, for his own nihilism often followed original lines. But Isabelle was essentially a mystic and no explanation confined within herself could content her for long. She was convinced of a meaning which, if she could perceive it, would explain the apparent chaos of her destiny.

The violent and seemingly gratuitous impact of Abdallah's destiny on her own, opened a perspective so unusual that she never formulated it to anyone except Sliman—who was long past astonishment—and spoke of it in her diary only with an extreme reticence. This was what she called 'the maraboutic question', and there can be no doubt that Isabelle did, from this time on, in a half-fearful way, believe herself destined—without any personal virtue, but simply because the Pen had so written at the creation of the world—to become a female marabout or perhaps one of the *Abdal*, the secret saints or pillars of Islam, a certain number of which, according to Moslem mystics, are destined to exist throughout the Moslem world in order to ensure liaison between heaven and earth. Such a destiny would be to the measure of the events which had hitherto composed the course of her life, and it, and it alone, could justify the destitution and unremitting suffering which she was convinced would form the rest of her existence.

If the idea took root at the moment of Abdallah's appearance beneath the hospital windows, it had probably been latent for some time and was perhaps less spontaneous than she believed. Si Lachmi—considered by a section of the Qadrya, as Abdallah himself testified at his trial, as 'second only to God' in the region—had admitted Isabelle as one of his most intimate disciples. Cheikh El-Hussein had been astonished at her Koranic learning and through him she had been able to pass the first night of the great Marabout's arrival with the little circle of his intimates, listening to the esoteric teaching which would be denied to the ordinary *khouan*. All three of the venerated sons of Sidi Brahim respected her and showed her continual marks of favour. For the mass of the initiates, such astonishing advancement for a European, a woman and a convert, could not be without some special significance. Most of them were ignorant and superstitious—astonishingly ignorant as so many Moslems are in the things of Islam—and it was only natural that the rumour began to circulate that Si

Mahmoud was a sort of saint. A number of holy men, not of maraboutic descent, were, in fact, regarded as marabouts during their lifetime and popular consideration was ready to credit the holy, the wise and even the mad with the title of marabout. The escape at Behima itself lent itself to the legend of divine intervention and several witnesses to the event were already swearing that they had seen a rosy cloud descend upon her and veil her from the assassin's sight.

The very fact of Isabelle's sex and male attire may have evoked in the minds of some the idea of maraboutism, even as it profoundly shocked others. Isabelle liked to believe that her masculine disguise concealed her identity; actually, her secret was no secret at all. The delicate courtesy of the Arabs admitted that, as she wished to pass for a man, she should be treated as such, but only strangers were deceived, and not for long.

Arab mythology contains a long tradition of female marabouts, several of whom had scoured the desert disguised as men. Lella Aouda ben Sidi Mohammed was one of the most famous examples, and centuries later men still spoke of the beauty and learning of the great chieftainess, her debauched early life and her pious end as a cave-dwelling hermit. Long after her there had been Lella Fatma, issue of a powerful maraboutic family who had organized the resistance against the French in the Djurdjura mountains in 1857. Like many of the famous marabouts, she had the gift of prophecy and had foretold the French victory and the details of her own capture. Riding in the desert of Southern Oran during the year of Isabelle's stay in El Oued, was an exquisite little saint affiliated to the Qadrya—the eighteen-year-old Dehbiya of the Sedjara tribe. In 1899 she had visited Oran, dressed in her habitual male costume consisting of two light burnous, a woollen haik, an abeyah and a kenbouch, her nails lightly tinted with henna as a concession to feminine coquetry. Dehbiya was venerated in her own region as one of the holiest female marabouts in Islam because of her skill in the science of ecstasy, which was held in great consideration among the Qadrya. She had become such an adept in this science and the mysterious methods taught by the sect that she would fall several times a day into a deep trance, during which she would pronounce the name of Sidi Abd-el-Kader Djilani 'in a voice of thunder', as the awed assistants reported.

Isabelle, then, although she denied exercising any religious influence among the tribes, may have heard herself spoken of among the Chaamba nomads and the primitive shepherds of the Rebaia whom she had doctored and cared for in the desert, as a marabout. The legend had grown up and she had paid no attention to it, but the shock of the adventure at Behima and the desire to find an inner meaning to this apparently incomprehensible affair may have brought it to her mind. She certainly did not see herself for a moment as a marabout, but simply began to ask herself whether she was not being prepared, according to the 'Mektoub' decreed by God and without any desire on her own part, for a state of sainthood or rather that unity with God which is the goal of Sufism.

These were the things which Isabelle confided to her journal but which remained completely unsuspected by her friends. One of the most intimate of them wrote after her death that he had never seen Isabelle show any special interest in religious matters and that, although she professed to be a Moslem, he had never known her to carry out the practices of Islam. Moreover, she was careful to mask her inner self. The street urchin side of her nature was that which she showed to the world and she showed it so thoroughly that, as the Algerian poet, C. M. Robert, wrote after her death:

'It is admitted everywhere in the country that she drank more than any soldier of the Foreign Legion, smoked more *kif* than a hashish addict and made love for the pleasure of it. . . .'

Yet at the same time as these colourful stories were being passed around the garrisons of the South, Isabelle was noting in her journal:

'God has sown certain fruitful seeds in my soul: complete detachment from the things of this world, faith, and a burning love, pitiful and infinite, for the suffering. . . .'

And again:

'The human body is nothing; the human soul, everything.'

At last the drains were removed from the wounded elbow, the fever began to subside and the severed muscle to knit up again. Isabelle could move her arm slightly, but could neither raise it nor make much use of the hand, and she expected to remain infirm for life from the accident.[1] Towards the end of February she took her first outing and, a few days later, rode with the doctor to Guémar, to visit Cheikh El-Hussein; the regained freedom, the air and exercise made her realize that the forebodings and spiritual agony of the weeks in hospital came largely from physical constraint and lack of liberty. She felt full of strength again, ready for the long journey to Batna, to rejoin Sliman, yet curiously nostalgic at the thought of quitting the hospital, with its peace and security, the talks and often heated discussions with the doctor, the jokes with the friendly soldier-nurses.

On February 25th, she left El Oued, riding on 'Souff' accompanied by Dr. Taste, and spent the night at the *zaouia* of Guémar. On the following day a guide brought her over the dunes to the point where she was to join a caravan composed of some natives of Guémar, a Spahi, an elderly woman, riding to Batna with her son and two madmen accompanied by a young Algerian guard. They rode slowly, with many halts, taking the rough track that passes by Chegga and making much of the journey on foot. When they rejoined the main route at Biskra, Isabelle was exhausted, but after a day's rest she set off by train for Batna.

Sliman awaited her there, but the reunion was incomplete. His regiment was confined to a certain quarter of the town, to which Isabelle was not allowed access, and he was seldom free

---

[1] Actually she recovered the use of her arm completely.

to visit her. Their happiness was confined to rapid, clandestine meetings at night by the ramparts, and Isabelle began to envy the lot of the cloistered Arab women, their complete dependence on their men and the security of their homes.

The time spent at Batna was perhaps the darkest of her life, for she had arrived practically destitute and was soon reduced to a misery which could hardly have been matched in the poorest of the native quarters. The town itself is one of the most depressing in North Africa, built for the convenience of the military in European style, streets and houses set in lines as rigid as those of a regiment on parade, surrounded by an immense, treeless plain. It was one of those bitterly cold springs which occasionally fall upon the warm Mediterranean lands and an icy rain transformed the town into a sort of bog. Isabelle had only light summer clothes and her shoes had long ceased to give any protection against the damp. Even poor Souff became ill under his new regime and she was deprived of the long rides over the mountains, on the slopes of the Aurès that reminded her, with their misty colouring of purple and blue, of the Jura and the Salève that rears its head into the clouds, high above Geneva. From day to day between the word sketches of her surroundings that she never failed to make, and the cries of nostalgia for the desert and for the peaceful life with Sliman which she confided to her diary, she noted in short phrases the progress of material misery:

'*March 28th.* Here it is complete destitution. . . . No food, no money, no fire. . . . Nothing!

'*April 26th.* The fact is that I now visit people exactly *in order to eat*, so that I may keep my health—a thing which would have seemed as *impossible* to me a little while ago as that other thing which I have also done: to seek out those enclosed and mysterious beings, the marabouts, and ask them for money. . . .'

There was an ironic side to this situation and Isabelle was perfectly conscious of it. Abdallah was to be tried in Constantine, since, living in a military area, he was to be brought before a court-martial. The *dossier* of the affair was being compiled with the unhurried meticulousness which characterizes French law. Isabelle's own rôle—which constituted an element at least as mysterious as the motives for Abdallah's apparently gratuitous act—was being thoroughly investigated and the police of Batna were kept busy compiling reports on her. She was quite aware of their activities and knew that the one thing which protected her from a persecution which might easily become unbearable was the fact that these reports, as well as the general rumour, constantly referred to her great wealth.

Two years earlier, at the time of her first journey into the Sahara, Isabelle had left Tunis with a sum of money which, if not considerable, was at least sufficient for all her needs. Instead of rationing herself prudently, she had spent without counting in Batna and Biskra, living the carelessly splendid life which seemed natural to the step-daughter of a Russian aristocrat once she had something in her pocket. The ever-watchful police had noted her in their files at that time as a wealthy eccentric in search of adventure, and in the official view she continued as such. If, instead of the splendid burnous she had worn in 1899, she was covered with clothes that were barely respectable and if, instead of the best hotels, she lodged poorly in the Arab quarter, it was presumably in search of copy or of disreputable adventures. The official mind, once made up, is practically impossible to change, and the simple explanation that she had no money was the only one which apparently occurred to no one. So while Isabelle starved and froze and awaited in hope and despair for Sliman's rare periods of leave, the files in Constantine were constantly swollen by reports on the curious activities of the rich Russian adventuress who passed herself off as Si Mahmoud Essadi. The policeman to whom she was obliged to report herself almost every day and who acted as a sort of spy on her activities, was an ill-disposed and brutal creature, but he was fortunately a tremendous snob. The legend of her riches kept his behaviour just within the bounds of official correctness. Isabelle was convinced that, if he became aware of the truth, his discreet persecution would give way to other and far more dangerous methods.

Isabelle had spent just two months in Batna when she was informed that the French authorities had decided to expel her from North Africa. No explanation was given, no official measure had been announced as yet; she was simply warned to leave the country immediately. As a Russian citizen, a foreigner, she had no recourse. An appeal to her own consul brought a cold refusal to intervene. Sliman, on whom his rank of sergeant in the Spahis had automatically conferred French nationality, could confer that nationality on her by marriage. He immediately applied for permission to marry—until the end of his period of service he was not free to do so without the permission of his colonel. The result was a flat refusal, on the excuse that a non-commissioned officer of the Spahis could not be encouraged to ally himself to a foreigner. Isabelle was too poor, too much at the mercy of ill-disposed officials, to be able to defend herself or even to take time to inquire into the exact nature of the proceedings against her. She could only pack her few miserable belongings in a bundle and take a fourth-class ticket to Marseilles.

'Sunday, May 5th, 9 a.m. In the midst of the terrible dislocation of my life during these last few days—darker than any I have ever lived through—I realize with joy the permanence of the sense of beauty, the love of art and of nature.

'I have come to this ultimate limit of misery which consists of hunger and destitution and a continual anguish for my material existence. I feel like some animal that is being pitilessly pursued, with the evident intention of killing it, annihilating it. I am about to be separated from that which I love most in the world, that which brightens the whole of my sad life—for my life has been *essentially* sad, since the beginning and for ever. I have known for years, with *certainty*, that I should arrive at this degree of misery.

'Yet, in the midst of all this, after all the partings, and face

121

to face with all the dangers, I feel that I shall not weaken, that two things remain intact: my religion and my pride, and that I am proud to undergo these sufferings that have nothing ordinary about them, to have shed my blood and to have been persecuted for the sake of a Faith.

'The life-force has not been annihilated in me. It will be prodigious and indestructible from now on, and my life, though bitter, dark and cruel, is yet neither colourless nor repulsive. There still remains the profound love of Rouh's essentially beautiful and beauty-loving heart, to brighten it from near or from far. And there is also the sentiment, per-haps even more subtle and more sincere, of art, of beauty, of nature. . . .

'There is beauty in everything and it is the poet's gift to be able to discover it. This gift is not dead in me and I am proud of that, for the only *unperishable* treasures are those of the mind. . . .

'While I was sitting like a tramp by the roadside, in com-pany with that humble, faithful and unconscious friend who is also going to be taken from me now, I felt like a great land-owner, watching the golden fields of flowering colza, the emerald of wheat and barley and the opal of the chihs with their intoxicating scent. Only the grave can take that wealth from me . . . and who knows, if the Mektoub allows me time to formulate a few fragments of it, perhaps it will survive me in the memories of a few people.

'*Only the superior forms of life are worth living*, and the im-becile and miserly millionaire and the society beauty, rich and adulated, would envy, *if they knew*, the miserable rags, the verminous lodgings and scanty food of her who has found the source of love (the only love that is possible and real since no question of vulgar advantages is mingled with it) and who is able to take proud possession of the whole vast universe and its mysterious heart, to possess it and revel in it more fully than any ancient autocrat could revel in his illusive power.'

Chapter Ten

ISABELLE sailed from Bône on 9th May 1901, on the steamship *Le Berry*. As women passengers travelling alone were not admitted to the painful promiscuity of the fourth-class deck, she travelled under the name of Pierre Mouchet, and described herself as a day labourer. The journey lasted four days, during most of which a furious storm raged. On disembarking, she went to the Rue de l'Oran, where Augustin was living with his wife and the little girl, Hélène.

Isabelle's period of resentment and disappointment over Augustin's failure to continue the alliance and the projects of their childhood had been partly dissolved by his sympathetic attitude towards Sliman. His first friendly letter on the subject had set her dreaming of a life *à trois*, in which Augustin would join Sliman and herself in Africa and help them to run a shop, a café, a plantation or anything else that seemed likely to bring in a quick fortune. Only the presence of the intrusive but unescapable 'Jenny' prevented her pressing him more actively to throw up everything and come to her. At the bottom of her heart, she despised him for having linked his life to that of such an essentially vulgar creature as her sister-in-law.

Meanwhile, she had nowhere else to go and was obliged,

whether she liked it or not, to lodge with the de Moerders. She found them in a state of poverty as acute as her own. Augustin was essentially incapable and family life had not endowed him with a sense of responsibility. There was barely enough to eat and, in face of the continual struggle for existence, Jenny revealed herself as hysterical and uncontrolled as she was pettily conventional. In the pathetic figure of the little girl she seemed to recognize something of herself, and this mysterious encounter filled her with pity and anxiety for the future of a child in that feckless and unhappy household. A few days in Augustin's company showed her that the old comradeship was really and irrevocably finished and that she must cease to look for comfort or understanding in that direction. Trophimovsky's prophecy, which she had rejected so furiously, returned to her mind and once more she was forced to recognize the extraordinary clear-sightedness of that strange philosopher.

Above all things, Isabelle desired to obtain money—enough to enable her to live in some sort of security with Sliman and to be less at the mercy of the enemies and detractors who took advantage of her poverty. She had hoped to have news of the Villa Neuve, but Augustin could only answer that things were still in the hands of M. Samuel. He was too incompetent to do anything but leave things indefinitely to this highly suspicious character. Isabelle herself could do nothing without going to Geneva, which was beyond her means. She spent her time miserably, noting every detail she could remember of the experience at Behima, of the journey up from the South, the leave-taking with Sliman and the terrible journey on the storm-battered *Berry*.

It seems that, since that day in May, when she had noted laconically in her diary: 'Yesterday evening, learned news of expulsion', she had realized that this news was false, or at least premature. She had been warned to leave, but the warning was less official than she had been made to believe, perhaps by those who had an interest in getting rid of her. Once in Marseilles she had learned that no order had yet been signed and that only lack of money need prevent her returning to Algeria. In fact she would be obliged to return, for she had received notice that Abdallah's trial was scheduled for July 18th and that her presence as a witness would be required.

The money arrived—enough for a fourth-class passage and sent perhaps by the authorities in order to enable her to attend the trial. On June 13th, she sailed for Bône, then loitered in the docks until she was able to negotiate a passage to Philippeville on the *Félix-Touache*, one of those more-or-less seaworthy little boats that touch in at the various ports along the North African coast.

On the deck, seated among the coils of rope apart from the other passengers, Isabelle noticed a young man whose aspect was so curious that it immediately caught her attention:

'Extremely thin, with a bronzed, beardless, sharp-featured face, he wore linen trousers that were too short for him, a sort of striped hunter's waistcoat open on his bony chest and shabby straw hat. His hollow eyes, of a changing, tawny colour, had a strange expression of mingled fear and savage defiance.'[1]

This man was Amara, a shepherd of the Ouled-Ali tribe, returning to conditional freedom after serving eight years' penal servitude at Chiavari in Corsica. During the long night on board, he told his story without reticence to the young Moslem labourer stretched out beside him on a blanket spread on the deck.

When he was eighteen, Amara recounted, his father had given him a fine grey mare, 'rapid as the wind and savage as a panther'. One day the mare disappeared and, after a long search, Amara discovered that she had been stolen by a shepherd of a neighbouring tribe. He complained to his cheikh, but when the police came to look for the mare, the thief, knowing that he could no longer sell her, cut her throat and hid the body in a chasm among the rocks.

When Amara learned of this, he resolved to take revenge

[1] 'Au Pays des Sables'

and, coming by night to the hut of Ahmed, the thief, he sur-prised him asleep beside his flock, with his head pillowed on his gun. He was able to snatch the gun and kill Ahmed, then, pursued by the dogs and men of the tribe, he escaped without being recognized into the hills.

His flight, and the story of the stolen mare, soon led to his discovery and after three days he was arrested and brought before the tribunal which spared him the death penalty on account of his youth but condemned him to deportation and the penal colony.

When Isabelle asked the ex-convict what he meant to do on his return, he replied:

'I shall stay with my father and work. I shall take our flocks out to pasture. But if ever I meet by night in a lonely place one of the Ouled-Hassein who had me arrested, I shall kill him.'

In the morning, they disembarked and took the train for Constantine:

'Amara watched the landscape that slid past us, his pupils wide with joy and a sort of astonishment.

' "Look!" he said to me suddenly. "Look: there is wheat . . . and over there, a field of barley. Oh, look, brother, there are Moslem women, gathering up the stones from that field. . . ."

'He was possessed by an intense emotion. His lips trembled, and, at the sight of the crops that are so loved and venerated by the Bedouin and the men of his race, Amara began to weep like a child.

' "Live in peace, like your ancestors", I said to him, "and your heart will be at peace. Leave vengeance to God."

' "He who cannot wreak vengeance stifles and suffers. I must revenge myself on those who have done me so much harm. . . ." '

Isabelle remembered this conversation and the story told during the sleepless night in the harbour of Philippeville and later published it as a short story entitled *Amara the Convict*. This young man's suffering in exile, his fear of dying and being buried, like so many of his companions of Chiavari, far from Islam, his rapture at the sight of his homeland, could not weigh against the almost physical need for vengeance. One day, perhaps almost immediately, he would meet one of the men of the hostile tribe and kill him. Then he would be arrested and pay for his act with his own life. But it would be Christian justice, foreign justice, that would condemn him. Amara himself could not conceive of his action as a crime.

And there in Constantine, Abdallah ben Mohammed was awaiting the sentence of the same justice, which in his eyes, as in those of Amara, was no justice at all. He too had obeyed a primitive and sacred instinct. He had hoped to kill in the name of God and his revenge was nobler than that of Amara because it was impersonal.

The trial took place on June 18th and caused a certain excitement in the region on account of the celebrated or picturesque persons called as witnesses. Isabelle was accompanied by Sliman, who had obtained leave to come to Constantine, and had the moral support of Si Lachmi, who had arrived by train on the previous day. Her own letter to *La Dépêche Algérienne* had aroused the curiosity of the Europeans and the result was that, where the crime itself had been passed over in utter silence, the trial was fully reported in the whole of the Algerian Press.

The account published by *La Dépêche Algérienne* on June 23rd (the colonial Press in those days treated such things in somewhat leisurely fashion) was perhaps the most complete and objective:

'The affair of the drama at Behima came before the court-martial at Constantine on Tuesday, June 18th. The audience was fixed for 7 a.m., and by half-past six the gallery was filled with a great number of the wives of officers and of civilian officials. We noticed the presence of General Laborie de Labattut and of most of the officers of the Constantine garrison.

'Mademoiselle Isabelle Eberhardt, who wore female native costume, was seated in the witnesses' room, awaiting the opening of the court.

'We also noticed the marabout Mohammed Lachmi, wearing a green burnous and a number of witnesses, all well dressed and who appeared to belong to the great tents of the Sahara.

'The President, M. Janin, Lieutenant-Colonel of the Artillery, declared the court open.

'The accused was brought in and the interpreter proceeded to establish his identity.

'The accused, Abdallah ben Si Mohammed, who was livid, could hardly speak. He stated that he was a trader at Behima but that he did not know the place or date of his birth.

'The witnesses were then called over.

'The clerk next read the accusation, which retraced the events which we have exposed, spoke of the eccentricities of Mademoiselle Eberhardt, who is engaged to a native quartermaster of the Third Spahis and who is affiliated to the sect of the Qadrya and had rendered various services to the venerated marabout of the sect. He also spoke of the rivalry between two religious sects and finally of the numerous aggressions to which French officers have fallen victim in the Touggourt region.

'The President then proceeded to interrogate the witness, who replied: "I did not strike a European, I struck a Moslem under a divine impulsion. One day I received a mission from God, who ordered me to go to the Djrid, passing by Behima, where I was to meet Mademoiselle Eberhardt, who created disorder in the Moslem religion. An angel also appeared to tell me that Si Mohammed el Lachmi, marabout of the sect of the Qadrya, would be proceeding to Tunisia and was accompanied by Mademoiselle Eberhardt, who wore masculine dress, which is contrary to our customs, and thus made trouble in our religion.

' "After receiving this divine impulsion, I fasted for five days without seeing my wife or my children. On the sixth

128

day, the marabout Ben el Lachmi arrived. Then I left my home to pay a visit to him who is considered in our country as a second God. The angel still pursued me, advising me to kill the European who troubled our religion. Then I took a sabre and I committed the crime you know of. At this moment, even if there had been a number of guns trained on me, they would not have prevented me carrying out this act. Now I feel differently and I ask the pardon of the woman I struck."

'Me. de Laffont: "What was the nature of the disorders provoked by Mademoiselle Eberhardt?'

'Accused: "She dressed as a man—that is what the angels and Sidi Abdelkader[1] told me. I also had a suspicion: I thought she was the mistress of the marabout El Lachmi. (Stir in court.)

'Mlle. Isabelle Eberhardt, 35 years,[2] born in Geneva, Switzerland: (The victim's deposition confirmed the account of the crime which she wrote and which we published in *La Dépêche Algérienne*.)

The President: "Is it not true that the accused has declared that he struck you for the love of God?"

'Answer: "That is a reply he has thought out. He knew that I am a Moslem and it was the first time I had ever been to Behima."

'The Government Commissioner: "The accused maintains that you created a disturbance in the Moslem religion."

'Answer: "He has changed his system of defence several times."

'The President: "Tell us if the wearing of masculine dress by a woman is considered as an insult to the Moslem religion?"

'Answer: "It is considered simply as improper."

'The President: "But why do you wear it?"

'Answer: "It is practical for riding."

'In reply to the President, Mademoiselle Eberhardt declared

[1] Founder of the Qadrya.

[2] *La Dépêche Algérienne* added eleven years to Isabelle's age. She was twenty-four at this time.

that she held no grudge against the accused and forgave him freely.

'Mohammed ben Abderrahman, cheikh of Behima: "The accused told me, on the day I arrested him, that God and the cheikh Sidi Abdelkader had ordained his act. This native, who is in possession of all his faculties, has always been honest and has never done any harm."

'The Government Commissioner: "Why did you not arrest the culprit immediately after the crime?"

'Answer: "I was not present at the time of the event, but as soon as I heard of it, I went to the house of the accused's father, who told me that his son was not at home and, as he insulted me and refused to hand over his son, I bound him."

'Me. de Laffont: "Is the cheikh informed of the infamous accusation which has been brought regarding the rivalry of the two sects?"

'Answer: "I have heard of it from the officer of the Judicial Police who conducted the inquiry."

'Me. de Laffont insisted on the cheikh giving his personal opinion, although he was still under the influence of the marabout, and not under the protection of his immediate superiors.

'At this point, Mademoiselle Eberhardt intervened indignantly and asked leave to speak, but Me. de Laffont protested, and remarked, addressing himself immediately to Mlle. Eberhardt: "We are in France here, not in Russia."

'The Government Commissioner asked the witness who, in his quality of cheikh, is the mandatory of French authority, why he had addressed himself to the marabout instead of arresting the aggressor.

'Answer: "If I had gone into the house, Abdallah would have killed me."

'Me. de Laffont: "This demonstrates the supremacy of the influence of the marabouts over that of the French."

'(Several witnesses now repeated the details of the crime, confirming Isabelle's account.)

'Mohammed ben Lakdar ben Mohammed, father of the

accused: "On the night before the crime, my son, who had been fasting for six days, drove his wife and children out of his house. As we were in the habit of going to greet Si Lachmi, I went to him that day with all the notable men of the district. If I had foreseen what was to happen, I should have bound my son hand and foot to prevent him committing the crime.

' "When I handed him over to the marabout, he was foaming at the mouth. He declared to me that he had been prompted by the cheikh and his servants and by a messenger from God. I went with the notable men of the district to implore the marabout's pardon, which he refused to me."

'(The Court adjourned at this point.)

'M. Martin, Government Commissioner, declared this is a time at which the Moslem world is being stirred by religious fanaticism, especially in the Souff, where numerous acts of revolt are taking place. (He cites a number of cases and concludes): "Criminals must not imagine that, because we respect all religions, we shall be indulgent when they say to me: 'It was God who commanded me to commit this crime.' "

'Speaking of the attempted murder, M. Martin recalled some of the declarations of the accused, for example: "The French have set over us in this country a cheikh and a khodja[1] who plunder us. It is for hatred of the French that I struck Mlle. Eberhardt, a Frenchwoman. It would not have been agreeable to God if I had struck a Moslem."

'Armed with this declaration, the Government Commissioner demanded the death penalty.

'Counsel for the defence pleaded eloquently for his client, blinded and hypnotized by fanaticism. He considered that Mlle. Eberhardt, who is rich, well educated and independent, could employ her talents more usefully than by affiliating herself to the sects of the South.

'The Council retired and returned with an affirmative verdict, mitigated by attenuating circumstances: attempted premeditated murder; hard labour for life. (Stir in court.)

'General Laborie de Labattut, who went over to Mlle.

[1] Secretary of the Administration.

131

Eberhardt to ask her impressions of the verdict, was heard to say to her: "You cannot say that French justice has not thoroughly avenged you!" '

Thus ran the report of the relatively liberal and objective *Dépêche Algérienne*. Other organs of the Algerian Press did not confine themselves to describing the course of the trial, during certain periods of which, it is true, one might have imagined that Isabelle, rather than Abdullah ben Mohammed, played the rôle of the accused.

During the short adjournment in the middle of the trial, Isabelle had left the court and gone to walk in the street with Sliman, seeking to calm her agitation. On returning, she had been handed a mandate of expulsion, which exiled her for ever from the French possessions in North Africa. The false alarm in Bône had become a reality.

She was prepared this time, almost resigned in advance. Before leaving for Marseilles, she made a declaration to the Press, knowing that it could have no effect on the decision of the authorities, but desiring to justify herself in the eyes of all those, ignorant or indifferent, to whom she would inevitably appear as a spy in the service of some unspecified foreign power, or at least as an undesirable alien. The text of the declaration ran:

'As I have already declared, both at the trial and in my two letters to the *Dépêche Algérienne*, I have and always shall have the conviction that Abdallah ben Si Mohammed ben Lakhdar was an instrument in the hands of others who had an interest, real or imagined, in getting rid of me. It is evident that even if, as he declared to his father at the time of his arrest,[1] he had been paid to kill me, Abdallah could not hope to profit from his crime, since he attacked me in an inhabited house and among people whom he knew to be my friends. Thus it is obvious that this man is a maniac. He has shown his repentance and asked my pardon, even during the trial. For these

[1] This detail was suppressed at the trial, or at least in the accounts of the Press.

reasons I find the verdict given to-day excessively severe and I wish to declare that I regret this severity. Abdallah has a wife and children. I am a woman and I pity this widow and these orphans with all my heart. As for Abdallah himself, I feel only the deepest pity for him. I was painfully surprised on leaving the court this morning, to learn that I am the object of a mandate of expulsion issued against me by the Governor-General. . . . I cannot understand for what reasons this measure has been taken against me, who am Russian and have a perfectly clear conscience. I have never taken part in nor known of any anti-French action, either in the Sahara or in the Tell. On the contrary, I defended the late naib of Ouargla, Sidi Mohammed Taieb, who died gloriously under the French flag, with all my force against the accusations of certain Moslems, ignorant of the real Islam—that of the Koran and the Sunna—who accused the Naib of having betrayed Islam by installing the French at Ain-Salah. I have spoken at all times and everywhere to the natives in favour of France, which is my adopted country. Then why should I be the object of a measure which, while deeply wounding to my feelings as a Russian, causes me immense pain of another sort, since it separates me from my fiancé who, as a non-commissioned officer in the garrison at Batna, cannot follow me? I could have understood if I had been forbidden to visit the military territory, in order to save me from the vengeance of Abdallah's tribe, but I have no desire to return to the South. I ask nothing but to be allowed to live at Batna and to marry the man who has been the companion of my ill-fortune and who is my only moral support in this world. That is all. . . . '

Chapter Eleven

IN her novel, *Trimardeur*, Isabelle Eberhardt painted a picture of Marseilles as she learned to know it during the miserable summer of 1901. It was the Marseilles of reeking slums, of hunger, drunken brawls and exploited labour. Augustin's Marseilles—for the book-loving son of the General of the Imperial Army could find no better means of existence than to engage himself as an occasional dock labourer on the quais of the Joliette or of Lazaret. There he worked, when he could persuade a foreman to hire him, among the dregs of half a hundred nations at a daily wage that barely held off starvation, discharging the ships that brought cargoes from North and West Africa, from the Middle East, from Indo-China and the East Indies.

Isabelle accompanied her brother and soon became familiar with the crude, vigorous life of these workers. They were of every possible physical type, but all were marked by a common misery. They wore blue linen trousers, stained with oil and tar, striped jerseys and wide red woollen sashes, like those of the Zouaves. They had a slang of their own, partly Provençal, partly pure sailor, spattered with Arab and Chinese— the language of the Mediterranean ports. Many of them were

Arabs who had settled in Marseilles in the illusory hope of earning enough money to buy a farm at home, or who crossed regularly from Algeria, bringing flocks of sheep to the slaughter-houses. Augustin, the ex-legionary, was on terms of easy intimacy with many of them and Isabelle found a consolation in their company, since she could speak with them of Africa and feel herself among Moslems, perhaps even discover fellow *khouans* wearing the chaplet of the Qadrya.

The dockers accepted her naturally enough and presently she obtained work among them, engaging herself as a stevedore-cum-pulley-maker on a lighter used by the sanitary service, at a wage varying from $1\frac{1}{2}$ to 2 francs a day. Her body was trained to hardship and she was as tall and strong as most of them, in spite of the weakness of the left arm, where Abdallah's sabre had sectioned the muscle. But above all, she joined them in their moments of leisure; at midday when they sheltered from the burning sun in the shade of the wharves and devoured their meagre lunches from greasy paper packets, spread to form a plate on the open hand. While they talked, she noted expressions, slang words, or simply the exotic names of the boats tied against the quai that appealed to her by the strangeness and richness of their syllables—San Ireneo, Carthagenia, Santa Maria Dolorosa, Corinthia, Elena Pronti. . . . She learned from them too of the conditions in which they worked. There were no union tariffs for these day labourers. The French workers had a certain solidarity among themselves, but they were at the mercy of the unscrupulous competition of the Italians. These arrived in an unending stream in overcrowded boats from the Peninsula, swarmed on to the docks, sought out their compatriots and immediately proposed their services at cut prices to the harbour foremen. They seemed to live on nothing, and wages went steadily down before their invasion.

The sharp, thieving *titis* of Marseilles, the Greeks and the sad-eyed Arabs spoke of these conditions with a fury that was tinged with resignation. They knew themselves to be the dregs of the working class, the good-for-nothings who could find nothing better to do and in whose fate no one was interested. They had tried strikes, but hunger had always got the better of them and it had been easy for the harbour-master to get rid of the ringleaders. Augustin himself seems to have been laid off for his too great influence among his comrades. The ex-anarchist must have remembered the reunions in Geneva, the assassination of Alexander II, the deportations in Russia and the inflammatory exhortations of *Le Révolté* to the exploited masses. But neither he nor his sister were cut out for action. They were too profoundly individualistic and, like Trophimovsky before them, too sceptical of humanity to be able to give themselves up to a social cause.

Trimardeur, which is partly a portrait of Augustin, but even more of Isabelle herself, is really a study of this incapacity for a social existence which characterized all the children of Madame de Moerder. It tells the story of a young Russian, named Dmitri Orschanov, a student at St. Petersburg and affiliated to an anarchist society. St. Petersburg, which Isabelle had never seen, bears in the novel a strong resemblance to Geneva and the Orschanovs' home to the Villa Neuve:

'At an early age (Dmitri) learned to dream in the silence of the great house or at the bottom of an immense garden which had grown to a forest where the child loved to lose himself for hours together. The nut trees, the mountain-ash, the sad holly trees, formed an inextricable jungle beneath the full-grown trees—the powerful oaks, the slender lime trees, the delicate birches with their silver trunks. A lake slept in the shadow, invaded by reeds, in all the uneasy mystery of stagnant water. The trees sloped downward, hiding the view. Then suddenly they came to an end and there was the great Volga, wide and slow, flowing in the sunlight.'

Read Rhône for Volga, and there is all Isabelle's girlhood. The Nihilists of the Rue de l'Arquebuse, Vera—under the same name—, Chouchia, live in its pages. Trophimovsky makes a brief apparition. But above all, there is the conflict of the conscience which she had undergone during the last visit to

Geneva and which Augustin must have known even more acutely before he abandoned the Villa Neuve. Dmitri abandons the anarchist cause, in spite of his sincere convictions and his love for one of his woman comrades. He leaves Russia at the hour of her greatest need, stigmatized as a traitor by his comrades, and assumes the rôle of an eternal wanderer, sinking voluntarily lower and lower in his need for evasion:

'On his return a sombre need for suffering had forced him to return down there, to the quarter of misery, alcohol and prostitution. He went there at present without any purpose, without any intention of studying or making propaganda: simply, he was drawn now to the sorrowful filth, feeling a torturing desire to allow himself to sink down into it, for ever.'

Was it now of the slums of Tunis during those months after the death of her mother, that Isabelle was thinking, rather than of the unknown misery of St. Petersburg? At any rate, many of the stages of Dmitri's journey are based on Augustin's odyssey—the farm in Savoy, Marseilles, the Foreign Legion. If the novel had ever been finished, Dmitri might well have become Andrei Antonoff, the hero of the short story entitled *The Anarchist*, the portrait of another Russian who fled from the life that others had sought to impose on him and found peace and happiness in Africa, and who is unmistakably Isabelle herself.

She was working at the novel as best she could in Augustin's flat in the Boulevard de la Mérentié, where 'Jenny's' hatred was rapidly destroying the last links between her and her brother. The household was almost starving and had no resources except the German lessons which Augustin gave when he could find an occasional pupil. Isabelle despised the couple's constant preoccupation with their material needs and their whole attitude to life bored and disgusted her, but she scraped together such few francs as she could earn at odd jobs of work or borrow from Arab dockers at the Joliette and gave them to her sister-in-law for their common expenses. If she could have afforded a woman's dress, she noted one day in her diary, she might have found work, but the expense was out of the question. The poverty in the Boulevard de la Mérentié was becoming so acute that she was sometimes unable to write to Sliman for lack of money to buy a stamp; in place of tobacco she smoked the leaves that fell in the streets from the plantain trees. Augustin pawned his coat and trousers, then little Hélène's coat. Isabelle had already pawned everything but the single suit of clothes she wore each day. Her solicitude for her brother and his wife did not spare her a series of terrible scenes and, to complete her misery, her health, which had resisted more trials than most men could have supported, suddenly failed. The exhausted body was racked with fever, colic and terrible pains in the kidneys. Nightmares tore her out of her sleep, sweating with agony. She longed for Sliman, and the news that he was in hospital at Batna with a serious attack of bronchitis threw her into a frenzy of despair. 'Yesterday evening', she wrote to him on August 1st, 'and thus before I learned from your letter that you were in hospital, I knew it already, *in a most mysterious way*. I had gone to bed in my usual state of mind and had been reading. As soon as I had put out the light, I was seized by a terrible anguish and the idea came to me with great clarity that you were very ill, that you had been taken to hospital.' She knew him to be suffering from tuberculosis; another year must pass before he would be free of the Army, and now she imagined him dying far from her before they could meet again.

Before her departure, it had been decided that she should do all she could to obtain a permutation for Sliman—that is, to find a comrade serving in a regiment in France who would be willing to exchange his place. Isabelle began to write letters, seek support, supplicate officers. Colonel de Rancogne, a gallant officer of the Spahis stationed near Marseilles, had promised his help, but the weeks were passing by and every day of absence was a torture. Isabelle bombarded the patient colonel with letters:

'You had the great goodness', she wrote one day in June,

'to accept my fiancé, the quarter-master S. Ehnni, in your regiment and even to do all you could to obtain for him a rapid and favourable solution.

'A few days ago, I suddenly received a letter from my fiancé announcing that, in spite of all his supplications, he had been removed to hospital with bronchitis. . . . My fiancé writes that he is much better now and only desires to come here as quickly as possible and take up his service. In spite of this, the regimental doctor has informed him that, in order to obtain convalescent leave, he must produce a certificate attesting his means of existence. My fiancé has refused this leave, declaring that he is coming to a new regiment and feels quite capable of taking up his service again. The doctor then told him that he will not discharge him except on convalescent leave and that, if he has no one to take care of him, he will keep him until the end of his engagement—that is, until February 1902! I am sure and certain that my fiancé's health is not in such an alarming state as he is constantly being told and that his illness —the result of all the worries and sorrow we have had to endure—would soon disappear if he could come here and regularize the unhappy situation in which, in spite of ourselves, we have been placed for nearly a year. May I say that this affair of the hospital and convalescent leave seems to me most extraordinary. Is it not the continuation of the measures that have already been taken against us?'

The exchange of letters continued. Sliman's state of health was the excuse continually evoked for preventing his departure, and Isabelle's suspicions of his officer's motives may not have been entirely unfounded. Colonel de Rancogne, however, was an intelligent and comprehensive colonial. He promised his help, stirred the slow-moving administration and held out a hope for the happy end in which Isabelle had almost ceased to believe.

The separation from Sliman was all the more painful because she was aware of the weakness of his character and terrified of the effect her absence would have on him. He wrote seldom and his replies to her own flood of passionate letters were short and banal. His chief preoccupation was to persuade her to change her costume, which he believed to be responsible for her bad reputation with the authorities. As she had no money in Marseilles, he proposed to do some shopping for her in Batna and urged her, for her part, to procure herself a wig to hide her cropped hair. Isabelle reacted violently:

'You cannot, in any case, buy European clothes, for you have no idea of what they cost and I formally forbid you to contract a pennyworth of debt. I do not want to hear any more about dressing as an Arab woman, either. You know me, and you know that I am ready to obey you in everything, but not to give in to you when you want to do something that is quite mad. All I can concede to you is to give up dressing as an Arab, which is, in fact, the only thing that might annoy the authorities.'

But there were graver subjects of dispute between them. There were Sliman's long silences and, when he wrote, certain incoherencies that led Isabelle to suspect that he had been drinking. After a week in Marseilles, she was already growing anxious:

'I am not pleased with you. It is eight days since you left me and five since you went to Batna and you have not written to me yet. Where do you think I can find the courage to support the misery, the solitude and all the trouble you know of? The only thing that could comfort me would be a letter from you. You see that I am thinking day and night about Zuizou.

'Why do you forget me? Write to me on Saturday at the latest. If I do not get a letter by Sunday at the latest, I shall conclude that you have forgotten me and that, in spite of all your promises, you are glad to be at Batna . . . and then—of what use would it be to struggle or wait patiently? I have no more strength or courage or desire to live. I only live for you and through you. If you forget me, I shall need nothing any more.'

A letter came at last to console her and immediately she set about making plans for the future. Sliman, with her help, was to become a sort of prototype of the Arab of the future, to force the respect of the Europeans and show them of what a Moslem can be capable. She reminded him that he was destined, through his association with her, to enter the society of officers and she begged him to study and prepare himself for his new rôle:

'Remember that by working along the lines I have traced for you, you will be working for all your Moslem brothers; you will be giving the Arab-hating and disdainful French the example of an Arab who has begun his career as an ordinary soldier in the Spahis and attained to an envied and respected rank by his intelligence and his industry. If there were many such Arabs in Algeria, the French would be obliged to change their minds about the *bicots*. That is the true way of serving Islam, instead of fomenting useless and bloody revolts that only serve as a weapon for the enemies of the Arabs and discourage honest Frenchmen who wish for the good of our brothers. . . .We two, who have a single soul, a single heart, a single will, can do more than anyone else if you will only follow the lines I lay down for you in this letter. . . .'

There follow recommendations for Sliman's reading—the works of Zola appeared to Isabelle essential, because of the author's understanding of the social problems of his time, although she deplored his atheism and warned Sliman against allowing himself to be influenced by this tendency. In fact, she sometimes suspected that his religious zeal might be less than her own, and urged him anxiously to continue in her absence all the practices of their confraternity:

'Count firmly on God if you wish to cause me *great joy*. *Every evening*, before you go to sleep, recite "There is no god but God" and ask Djilani to help and protect us. . . . In this way our two souls will be united in prayer even when we are far from each other.'

But Sliman's next letter was disappointing. He seemed to pay no attention to her exhortations, did not in fact even refer to them, and contented himself with feeble complaints about Batna, his inadequate pay and life in general. Isabelle found his letters disconnected and incoherent, and noticed angrily that he did not even answer any of the important questions she had put to him:

'I am here—sad, exiled, penniless and powerless to prevent my family taking the road to destruction,' she wrote to him. 'All my thoughts are fixed on Batna, where is my only reason for living, my unique hope.

'Why is it that I do not weaken? Why should it be I, a "weak woman", who remains brave and struggles desperately? I have to go round the cafés frequented by Arabs and write their letters in return for a few sous or for tobacco. I have never failed, in all my letters, to speak to you as a *mother*, as a *brother*, to preach the true doctrine to you, to remind you that we are Moslems and *khouans*, that we have a part to play and a sacred aim in life; that despair and lack of resignation, lack of courage, indeed, are so many blasphemies. . . .

'Yes, indeed, I am your wife before God and Islam. But I am not a vulgar Fatma or an ordinary Oucha. I am also your brother Mahmout, the servant of God and Djilani, rather than the servant of her husband that every Arab woman is. I will *not admit*, do you hear, that you show yourself unworthy of the splendid dreams I have made for both of us and of which I told you only a part in my letter of last Tuesday.'

So the correspondence continued—fluent and agitated on Isabelle's part, brief and complaining on Sliman's.

Meanwhile, in the miserable room in which she found a precarious refuge from Jenny's nagging, she continued to write, forcing herself to forget Sliman for a while. The 'processus of literary creation' was really her only consolation now, as she had declared it to be in a period of depression in Bône, four years earlier. There was also the rather vague belief that she might solve her material difficulties by the sale of stories and articles. Lydia Paschkoff, half-admiring and half-patronizing her young disciple, continued to send letters of advice. She knew everyone and had an amiable mania for introducing her acquaintances to each other. Among the many relations she had proposed to Isabelle in Paris, had been the celebrated young dramatic author, Eugène Brieux, an ardent Socialist whose plays—*Blanchette, La Robe Rouge*, etc.— were so many cries of indignation against the injustice of society towards those whom it had itself disinherited. The colonial system, and especially certain methods and conceptions of the French administration of Tunisia and Algeria, roused his anger. Isabelle, first intimidated and then revolted by her brief insight into the literary life of Paris, had let slip many opportunities and her letter of introduction to Brieux was among those she had neglected to present. He had heard of her, however, was aware of her rôle in North Africa and believed that she could do much to support the cause of the natives.

Brieux was at this time in Nice, and Lydia urged the utility of an encounter. The state of Isabelle's wardrobe was unfavourable to an expedition to the Riviera, but she wrote explaining her situation and submitting two stories. Brieux— a good comrade in practice as well as in theory—sent a hundred francs with a promise of a further hundred francs each month for three months, and gave a favourable judgment on the stories. He made reserves, it is true, and in reply to Isabelle's anxious query whether she had originality, answered decidedly that this quality was not to be expected at her age. All he would admit was that she had chosen her models well and might in time develop a personality of her own, but he offered more positive encouragement by submitting a number of sketches of Tunisian life to *L'Illustration*, with his own warm recommendation. For the first time, Isabelle had a serious chance of breaking into the Parisian Press and establishing herself as a professional journalist.

L'Illustration refused her articles and Brieux, furious, cursed all reactionary reviews. He was persuaded, not only of Isabelle's talent, but of her unique opportunities, which he reproached her for systematically neglecting. As a Moslem, he wrote, she should come out squarely as the defender of her brothers in Islam, attack those who exploited them, expose the conditions of their life. Isabelle agreed with him wholeheartedly, but she knew herself too well and understood too clearly her own congenital disability to undertake any sustained and ordered action, to imagine herself in the rôle of politician:

'At first it was the monotony of this life that disgusted me', explains Dmitri Orschanov in *Trimardeur*. 'Then, almost unconsciously, I began to rebel against the *obligation* to be a man of social action that was imposed on me by the *milieu* in which I lived. I thirst for liberty, Gourieva, and I found no liberty among our libertarians.'

Dmitri-Isabelle was made for dreaming and solitary wandering. Brieux, like Vera, saw in her the anarchist, the warm human being with an outraged sense of justice, but they both ignored the Moslem and knew nothing of that inner voice which repeated, in counterpoint to their urgings towards action: If my brothers are poor and exploited it is because poverty and sadness are written in their destiny, and written by God himself.

The summer passed by, in these literary hopes and disappointments and in the sheer struggle for existence. Brieux's money had gone in paying off an old debt to Augustin and in buying clothes for the approaching wedding. Isabelle, having agreed to dress as a woman for the occasion, was taking quite an interest in her outfit and wrote to Sliman a detailed description of the black skirt, lilac satin blouse and black hat trimmed with lilacs which she was preparing for the occasion. As her hair was unlikely to grow in time, she even agreed to purchase a wig and sent out to Batna, pinned to her letter, a sample of jet black false hair—the cheapest on the market—on which she desired his opinion.

As autumn drew near, the news from Africa became more cheerful. Colonel de Rancogne had been active, Sliman persistent. The improvement in the young Spahi's health made it difficult to find a justification for keeping him in hospital or to maintain that the climate of France would aggravate his condition. At last Sliman announced his arrival. There were delays, agonizing incertitudes, but on August 28th he disembarked from the *Ville d'Oran* to join de Rancogne's regiment.

There was no further impediment to the marriage which Isabelle desired so much, but there were still endless formalities to be gone through. The couple took a miserable room in the rue Grignan and settled down to wait as patiently as they could. Sliman's pay, insufficient in Algeria, was negligible in France and the misery of Batna, in the fraternal atmosphere of Islam, was nothing compared to the misery of Europe. Endless scheming and borrowing of small sums from Arab porters and dockers as wretched as themselves hardly sufficed to keep them alive. 'Eden-Stony-broke' she baptized their temporary and unappetizing home, in memory of a legend scrawled by some sceptical legionary over the lintel of a crumbling hovel in the Sahara, which she had noted in passing and which appealed to her because it accepted and mocked at misery. It was the first of a number of homes which were to bear this title, all too aptly.

The marriage was celebrated, first in the Town Hall and then at the Mosque in accordance with the Moslem rite, on 17th October 1901. Sliman was of French nationality, in accordance with the law by which certain Algerians, and notably those holding a certain rank in the Army, automatically became citizens of the Metropolis. The legalization of their union thus made a Frenchwoman of Isabelle and she could no longer be excluded from any of the French colonies. Even so, the time of exile was not yet finished, since Sliman was obliged to pass the rest of his period of engagement in the Army in Marseilles. Winter brought icy winds roaring down the valley of the Rhône but, once more, there was no money to buy fuel and the couple were forced to accept a gift of wood from an acquaintance whom they distrusted. Sliman, disconsolate and homesick, detested this alien charity and called down the curse of Allah on the infidels and their mentality.

Sometimes the thought of Geneva returned to Isabelle with an intensity that she had never yet known. It was the lake, the misty outlines of the Jura that she saw in her dreams, and above all, the garden of the Villa Neuve, in spring, at the time when it was fragrant with lilac and the nightingales sang all night among the rose bushes. The capacity which she discovered in herself for taking leave of the present and recreating the past made the monotonous months of privation almost agreeable. A distant trumpet call from the barracks was enough to evoke, not only the memory of the Souff, but the actual sensation of the desert—the windy heat, the whiteness and great spaces where the fine sand whirled in the air like a pricking mist in the rider's face. While her spirit roamed in the bosky garden of Meyrin, in the palm-shaded oases of El Oued, she could forget the nagging worries and the mounting debts. With Sliman, 'the indispensable companion', beside her participating daily more and more deeply in her inner life, she relived the past, constantly astonished by the immense importance of certain moments which, at the time of their occurrence, had appeared insignificant and passed almost unnoticed:

'Ah! If only we could foresee, at each hour of our life, the capital importance of certain acts, even certain words, which appear to be negligible and indifferent! Such examples lead one to the conclusion that there are *no moments* in our life that are indifferent or without significance for the future.'

If it was, above all, the life at the Villa Neuve that she relived with this singular intensity, it was because the old home no longer existed for her in reality. Shortly before her marriage she had at last received news from the lamentable Samuel, who had systematically ignored, for years, both her own letters and those which she obliged the spineless Augustin to

146

write. Now he informed her that the villa had actually been sold for 30,000 francs. It was the moment she had been waiting for ever since the death of Trophimovsky and on which she had counted to bring her in the small sum which would enable her to create some sort of solid basis for her errant life. Disillusion followed swiftly in the form of a letter from her lawyer, announcing that, after all costs had been paid, she remained a debtor for the sum of sixty francs. The Villa Neuve—by now in such a state of abandon and decay that the new owners were forced to tear down and rebuild the greater part—had gone from her life with all its beloved memories and with it went the last reasonable hope of a less tormented future.

The House of Islam was open to her once more, but she must enter it in the guise of a vagabond, in rags, and hardly daring to make plans for even the immediate future. Sliman was due to leave the Army on February 20th. His health was frail, his education deficient. The couple could foresee no way out of their difficulties, no way to earn even the tiny sum which would keep a roof over their heads and pay for tobacco and a little food. Sliman's family lived in Bône and were willing to lodge them, but they, too, were poor and unlikely to appreciate such an unorthodox daughter-in-law as Isabelle. Their hospitality provided a momentary solution and they decided to go to Bône. Isabelle, at least, had the firm conviction that everything would be well once she was again on African soil. As for the making of plans—her destiny, like Sliman's, was already written in God's own handwriting and no amount of scheming would alter it.

At the turn of the year, Isabelle bid good-bye to Augustin and Jenny with no desire ever to see either of them again, and sailed with Sliman for the last time from Europe.

Chapter Twelve

At Bône the couple lived for a month in the promiscuity of an Arab household, where the parents were far from pleased at the added expense. Sliman, who had been as nonchalant as any nomad at El Oued, a true son of the desert and entirely under Isabelle's influence, began to show the indecisiveness and weakness of his character, to betray indeed some of the decadence of the town Arab. His liberation drew daily nearer, but the 'freedom from the slavery of the Army' which Isabelle had so often longed for, became a source of added anxiety now that it was in sight. The Army at least had fed him and provided a meagre wage. Now he would have to find work. Isabelle, energetic as ever when she had some immediate goal in sight, set out to coach him up to the standard required from a minor employee in the Government service.

This standard was not high, but poor Sliman was no apt pupil. He could read and write in French and Arabic, and that was almost all. Isabelle started him on a course of reading. enlarging his vocabulary by a daily ration of Pierre Loti. His admiration for the French novelist's romantic evocations of the desert equalled her own, and *Mon Frère Yves* brought tears to the eyes of the sensitive Spahi. Yet his progress was slow. His mind was tuned to the study of the Koran and the Sunna, to drowsy meditation among the blue smoke of the *kif* pipe, rather than to European learning. Isabella began to suspect that the great plans she had cherished for him as the champion of Arab rights, respected by the French for his learning and character, would be harder to carry out than she had imagined. The hero of the Sahara had begun to reveal himself, even while she was awaiting him in Marseilles, as inadequate for the rôle. Admiration began to give place to a pitying tenderness, and Isabelle realized once more that she was essentially alone.

February 20th arrived and Sliman was delivered of the gay red cloak and the high boots of the Spahis. The couple removed to Algiers: the lessons of arithmetic, spelling and geography continued in the rue de la Marine, in a sordid room, the cheapest that could be found in the town, that Isabelle baptized once more with the ironic name of 'Eden-Miseria'. She was almost accustomed by now to a life of extreme poverty, to borrowing the money for a meal and to furtive expeditions to the pawnbroker's, but Sliman had lived under the protection of the Army and found the régime of civilian liberty hard to support. He was not especially intelligent and, far from sharing Isabelle's taste for travel and adventure, he dreamed only of a small job in some comfortable corner, with a settled wage and no further worry. While he was out of work, he would no doubt have been quite content to pass his time in smoking and dreaming, but Isabelle forced him to study. She was the strong one now, on whom he leaned, and there was much of the mother and child relationship between them. Isabelle's 'absolute dependence' on her beloved Rouh' was of a strictly sensual order and perhaps already declining. In all practical matters it was she who guided, counselled and encouraged. She herself was working more systematically than she had ever done. Her short stories, her notes and sketches from El Oued, were polished and repolished; *Trimardeur* was drawing to a close. Several short stories had been accepted by the local press, but the payment was miserable and was always promptly swallowed up by her numerous creditors. Eugène Letord, whose friendship had never failed her, gave what he could spare, but there seemed to be no way out of the hopeless maze of poverty.

It was at this moment, when the future had never looked darker, that Isabelle made the acquaintance of Victor Barrucand, editor of the daily paper *Les Nouvelles*, a journal subsidized by a certain Senator Gérente and existing largely to further his electoral interests. During the preceding year, Isabelle had sent two stories, *Moghreb* and *Printemps au Désert*, which had been accepted and published. But Barrucand had done more for her; his had been the only voice in the Algerian Press that had been raised to protest against her expulsion from North Africa. On 27th June 1901, he had published a leader, under the heading: 'A drama of the South', in which he reproduced Isabelle's declaration to the Press and added:

'It is hard to understand why a mandate of expulsion should have been issued against this unfortunate woman. . . . Mlle. Eberhardt's ideas may perhaps shock our timid and well-trained instincts, but there is nothing in them which should be condemned. She has already been punished severely enough by her misadventure, without our straight-laced Administration inflicting a moral torture which is yet harder for her to bear.'

Barrucand's own tastes and opinions had drawn him to Isabelle before they ever met. He was a disciple of Bakunin and of Tolstoy, an ardent propagandist for the League for the Rights of Man. He campaigned, as far as the interests of his director and the prejudices of the Administration would allow him, for a more equitable treatment of the natives and managed to make himself exceedingly unpopular with the colonists. He was a man of letters too, with literary ambitions and had produced an unsuccessful drama and a novel entitled *Avec le Feu*, besides collaborating with the advanced reviews published in the colony, like *La Revue Blanche* and *La Grande France*. He was, in literature, an adept of the Parnassian School, put Beauty before all other considerations and loved the fine word and the purple passage. Enlightened European circles considered him, however, chiefly as a successful publicist and reproached him with seeking electoral support by publishing sensational news that was not always true. He probably had more enemies than any other man in Algiers.

Isabelle announced her visit at a moment when he was contemplating resigning from the editorship of *Les Nouvelles*, where he was in growing disaccord with Gérente, and founding a paper of his own, to be published in French and Arabic on alternate pages and designed to appeal to the lettered classes among the natives. He saw at once the use to which he could put Isabelle, with her unparalleled knowledge of native ways and her relations with circles usually closed to all Europeans. Her style, with its bluntness and occasional naïvety, was the very opposite of that which he usually admired, but he saw in her stories 'the promise of talent and, better still, a number of important observations'.

Isabelle and Barrucand thus knew each other fairly well by reputation, but the first personal contact was surprising to at least one of them. Barrucand had accepted without question the legend of the wealthy and eccentric Russian—which Isabelle herself had done nothing to correct—and had described her in these terms in his article. Yet when she arrived at the Villa Bellevue, in one of the pleasant residential suburbs of Algiers, he saw before him—since she was still keeping the promise made to Sliman of renouncing Arab dress—'a pale schoolboy, in a thin suit of blue cloth', bearing every sign of sickness and poverty.

Whatever may be said against Barrucand's subsequent conduct, he was a good friend to Isabelle during the rest of her life. At this first visit he accepted her as a regular contributor to *Les Nouvelles* and outlined to her his schemes for the new journal *Akhbar*, in which he had already decided that she should play an important rôle. Her personality intrigued him at once. The drawling voice, the equivocal clothes, the endless cigarettes and the street-urchin slang of his new protégé appealed to the self-conscious anarchist in him, and his interest was not less sincere because he saw that she might become a useful card in his hand.

Isabelle, on her side, was agreeably impressed on the whole. The editor, she noted, had a sharp, subtle mind, essentially modern, though she regretted he was typical of the time by his materialistic mental attitude. She felt sorry for him because he had recently lost his wife and was evidently unhappy, and admired his positive spirit and the capacity to adapt himself to life, which she felt herself to lack so notably. A little later, when she knew him better, she added severely that he was a dilettante in ideas and, above all, sensations, and applied to him the epithet which she had used long ago to describe the inhabitants of the Villa Neuve—'a moral nihilist'.

Yet in spite of this mental reserve, Isabelle was happy in Barrucand's company and in that of certain Arab intellectuals to whom he introduced her. She spent much time at the lovely villa, dreaming and scribbling among the scented trees of its garden and making endless plans with her editor for the new review. Barrucand paid her miserably for her articles, but promised better things for the future and meanwhile introduced her to useful acquaintances, procured free travel passes for her and published notes and stories which she hoped would one day attract the attention of some powerful journal in Paris.

The more he saw of his new assistant, the more intrigued he became. The intelligence and personality of this inexplicable creature enthralled him; he believed everything she told him, and soon affection and admiration grew to a sort of romantic idealization of her person. The picture he made of her resembled a sort of nymph of the desert rather than the unreliable and uncontrolled Isabelle of reality. Yet, strangely enough, he never fully appreciated her literary talent, considering her style as flat and her images as lacking in colour.[1]

Yet even Barrucand's admiration could not blind him to

[1] Barrucand's preface to *Dans l'ombre chaude de l'Islam* shows how unreal was his conception of her.

the fact that Isabelle was uncommonly difficult to work with. If not congenitally lazy, she was averse to making any regular effort. She could force herself only with difficulty to any action which did not arise from inner necessity and no writer ever depended more on inspiration or was more incapable of disciplining himself to a daily routine.

When she was happy, or when she was suffering from that 'fruitful melancholy' which was so often her mood, she felt a vivid impulsion to note her impressions, both objective and subjective. When, on the other hand, she was passing through a period of heavy depression, or when she was harassed by hostile circumstances, it was almost impossible for her to write. It was hard for her to accept the discipline of journalism, though she was proud to be able to care for Sliman. Luckily, the notebooks she had carried with her during the days when she could wander freely in her beloved Souff were so full of unused notes that they provided, with a little polishing, material for more articles than *Les Nouvelles* could use. Even so, her articles arrived irregularly, and she could not be persuaded to write except when she was in the mood.

However, there were consolations, and it was Barrucand who made it materially possible for her to visit Bou-Saada, where an introduction from a notable *khouan* of the Qadrya would open the doors of the famous *zaouia* of El-Hamel, where dwelt the woman marabout, Lella Zeyneb.

This journey had been long dreamed of and planned for. It was to be partly a spiritual retreat and partly a temporary escape from Algiers—that Algiers 'dishonoured by its population' which Isabelle hated more each day; the Algiers of the degenerate town Kabyles in their European clothes, the Algiers to which Europe had made the gift of all its vices without imparting any of its qualities of thought or culture. Bou-Saada, lying across the Plain of Hodna at the foot of the mountains of the Ouled-Naïl, was not yet of the Sahara, but at least it was far from the abject crowd, 'enemy of all dreams and all thought', product of that 'dirt-ridden, evil and imbecile civilization', which represented for Isabelle, as it must have done to the old misanthrope Trophimovsky, the lowest form of human existence.

So it was with the delight of a prisoner unloosed that Isabelle set off on her journey, at 7.50 a.m. of a cloudy day, with rain threatening.

The train carried her swiftly to Bordj-Bou-Arreridj, where she had alighted once before on the way to the South. Now the annex of El Oued was closed to her, the Souff forbidden territory. There was a moment's pang of regret, soon lost in the pleasure of the journey in a rickety old diligence that rumbled through the night over the stony track down to M'sila. A strong sirocco was blowing, so that the air blew hot and damp and the sky was full of low-hanging reddish clouds. Sometimes the route ran beside a sinuous wadi, bordered with oleander, sometimes it crossed reeking salty marshes and sometimes passed by half-ruined villages of dried clay. M'sila, where she arrived, exhausted, at three o'clock in the morning, was a dilapidated little town built on either bank of a deep, stony wadi. Its clusters of humped tombs and shaded gardens, reminded Isabelle poignantly of the Oued 'Rir and the Sahara, but the night, passed in the courtyard of the mosque, bathed in moonlight, was made hideous by swarming fleas and rest was impossible. Isabelle awoke her travelling companions before dawn and they set out again, she riding on a grey mare so clumsy that she soon preferred to walk barefoot through the *sebkha* until a mule could be procured at Baniou.

Bou-Saada appeared in a flourish of greenery against the background of arid, reddish coloured hills. A sinuously curling wadi formed a boundary for half the town, and flowering oleanders filled its bed in place of water. The blocks of houses, built on sloping, uneven ground, were gashed by ravines filled with greenery and gardens of vines and fig trees, oleanders and purple-flowering pomegranates. There were plantations of mulberry trees, cultivated by the Administration, and acacias with flowers that appeared like tiny yellow balls. Isabelle noticed how fine bred and delicate-limbed were the Saharan camels that knelt before the house of the Cheikh, but compared the women, with their huge, flat head-dresses, un-favourably with those of the Souff. They were closely veiled, but the young girls, who might still go uncovered, had wild, pale faces, thickly tattooed with tribal markings. The men seemed to her at once servile and brutal.

Bou-Saada, like the annex of El Oued, was under military control and Isabelle was nervous of the reception she was likely to meet. Her previous experiences with the Arab Bureau had rendered her cautious and she was anxious to do nothing to offend the French officers. When she presented herself at the Bureau, however, she realized at once that, not only had the Administration not been advised of her arrival, but they had no idea who she was. A permit to visit El-Hamel was granted without question by an affable officer, who had probably never heard of Behima or the Constantine trial.

She rode out before dawn, impatient to see the marabout, the mysterious woman who was spoken of with awe and reverence throughout every corner of Algeria where the *khouans* of the Rahmanya were to be found. Lella Zeyneb was the daughter of the powerful cheikh Sidi Mohammed Belkassem and had inherited his *baraka*, remaining virginal and austere to reign over the famous *zaouia*. Perhaps this visit to the living saint—her sister, since a woman, a Moslem and learned in the Koran—would be a revelation, show her the path that she herself must follow. . . . Perhaps she would impart some secret that would calm her own tormented spirit and enable her to discover 'the true meaning of the world, that which is for ever intangible and unknown . . . the abso-lute face of the world, which, if one could discover it, would be the face of God'. For Isabelle, every journey had a *possible* goal in the discovery of the Absolute.

So she rode, full of hope, through the lightening dusk, till dawn broke and showed her the brownish mauve hills, pitted like great faces marred with smallpox, rising to the left and, on her right, the plantations of date palms and the gardens intersected by low walls of dried mud. The road followed the bed of the wadi, passing under two great arches, hollowed out of reddish clay, their curve so low that she had to bend close over her horse's neck to pass beneath them.

Soon El-Hamel came in sight, overlooking a great cemetery that filled the valley with its innumerable tombs. Isabelle was surprised by the size and prosperous appearance of the village, which seemed incongruous in that savage landscape. The houses had high walls, coated to half their height with smooth clay, the upper half showing the design of clay bricks. They appeared to the traveller like Babylonian palaces, with their flat terraces looking over courtyards constructed with geometrical precision and gardens full of fruit trees. The *zaouia*, blue-domed like all those of the region, was built on a hill, a little way from the village, and beside it stood the mosque, newly built, surmounted by a great round dome. It was surrounded by other smaller cupolas and contained the tomb of Sidi Mohammed Belkassem, where a constant stream of pilgrims prostrated themselves in homage. Behind it, the mountains stretched away, range upon range, great tracts of rock, almost terrifying in their utter barrenness, melting at last in the distance to a transparent blue that faded into the sky.

Lella Zeyneb was absent and would return later in the day. Meanwhile, Isabelle visited the mosque. A little group of *khouans* was there, seated in a circle, according to the custom of the Rahmanya when at prayer, reciting the *dikr* of the Confraternity.

'There is no God but God.'
'O my God, may your grace fall on our Lord Mohammed, on his family and his companions and on him be blessing.'

After a time, other *khouans* entered and took their place, for at El-Hamel, as in many *zaouia* of the Rahmanya, the system of incessant prayer was practised, the *khouans* relaying each other, hour by hour, day and night, so that the name of God should not cease for an instant to be proclaimed in the *mesjed*.

The Rahmanya, indeed, was among the most fanatic of the Islamic Orders, and no other cheikhs made more exigent demands on their followers. It had been founded at the beginning of the eighteenth century by Si Mahmed-ben-abd-er-Rahman-bou-Qobrin, who demanded of his *khouans* that they should 'break down all their intellectual faculties in the service of God and become in the hands of their cheikh like a corpse in the hands of the corpse-washer'.

The *zaouia* of the order were spread over the whole of Algeria and its *khouans* were the most numerous of all the confraternities of North Africa. Its marabouts had been found to be concerned in almost every insurrection against the French since the beginning of the century, but two of its branches had remained loyal. One was at Tolga, the other that of El-Hamel, where Sidi Belkassem had been a firm friend to the French and their ally on more than one occasion. His influence had been immense, since he was considered in the region, and even far to the South, as a great worker of miracles. The Rahmanya related, for instance, that he had held up, by supernatural means, the train in which he was travelling, in order to say the prayer of the *'acer* in peace, and that the mechanics had been unable to proceed until the saint had finished his orisons. This event had taken place quite recently, a short time before his death, and had been sworn to by a number of reliable witnesses. His daughter was believed to have inherited his powers and the respect of the *khouans* of the region was mingled with a sort of reverence and tenderness because of her sex and the mystery of her secluded life.

Lella Zeyneb was now a woman of about fifty. Her manner was timid and gentle, like that of other women who have passed their lives in the harem, yet she had about her an air of authority. Her father had trained her from childhood to fill the rôle that awaited her, so that visitors realized at once that they were in the presence of a great cheikh. She received Isabelle kindly, as an honoured *khouan* of a friendly order, and spoke to her of the spiritual questions which tormented the young European. Isabelle, seated opposite the marabout on a sort of mattress, was moved by the pale, drawn face of her hostess, that told of a lifetime of fasting and asceticism. The soft, rather hoarse voice was interrupted now and again by a harsh cough that shook the frail body, fragile as that of a child under its burnous and veils.

Isabelle never revealed the conversation with Lella Zeyneb and only noted in her diary that she had come from it with a feeling of rejuvenation and renewed force. She spent the night in the hostelry of the *zaouia*, in a great room with a ceiling arched and domed in the style of the South, magnificently carpeted, but furnished only with three beds—a concession to European taste which annoyed her—a table and a few chairs. One window looked out over the cemetery, and the three others opened to the East, on to the wild and sinister mountains of the Ouled Naïl, and all night the walls were shaken by a tremendous storm.

Early in the morning, Isabelle returned to Bou-Saada. The visit to El-Hamel had passed as swiftly as a dream, and perhaps it had something of the unsatisfactory quality of a dream. She had expected some sort of absolute assurance from this woman who had made the renunciation which she herself sometimes longed to make. She had received from her comfort and encouragement in her faith, but the great Question still remained unanswered.

At Bou-Saada, she revisited the Arab Bureau, where she found the captain still amiable, still unconcerned with her identity. Then there was an interminable journey in an ancient diligence, crowded with voluble Jews wearing side-locks and caftans, their sloe-eyed wives loaded with ornaments of gold and silver filigrane. A day and a night passed in this bone-shaking vehicle, in which she sought in vain to find space for a moment's rest, until they reached Borj Bouira and the railway.

In Algiers, Sliman was waiting for her with great news. Barrucand had been busy in their interests and had recommended him for a post of *khodja*, or Arab secretary and interpreter, that had fallen vacant in the commune of Tenes, situated on the coast some hundred miles to the west. Isabelle must have asked herself if Barrucand's influence or Lella

Zeyneb's intercessions were responsible. At any rate, here was the first hope of material security which the couple had ever known. There was still a pitfall before them. In order to obtain the post, Sliman would have to pass an examination and pass elementary tests in a number of subjects. The ex-Spahi had done his best, and gallantly remained awake over the textbooks of history and grammar which Isabelle forced him to absorb, but his education still left much to be desired. There were three crowded days in Algiers, then the couple set off together to interview the mayor and corporation of the little town.

Chapter Thirteen

ARRUCAND's influence prevailed, Sliman obtained the post and he and Isabelle were soon installed in a relatively comfortable house in Tenes. At first sight, the little town appeared entirely charming, for it was situated near the coast, at the spot where the Wadi Allala wound down to the sea through the wild, romantic maze of rocks and caverns that guarded the entrance to the fertile valley of the Cheliff. The native town, constructed by the Phoenicians who traded with France and along the African coast from its tiny harbour, was surrounded by vegetable gardens and terraced vineyards, and beyond them, great stretches of fragrant pine forest swept along the stretch of the dunes. For Isabelle, who loved only the South with its austere white sands, and nomad people, this lovely, wooded country was too pretty, too civilized, to be other than a land of exile, but it offered security, the quiet life which suited Sliman's failing health and the opportunity of observing the manners and customs of certain Berber tribes yet unknown to her. It was with a feeling of relief and thankfulness that she installed her few belongings and set out with Sliman to make the acquaintance of his new colleagues.

The round of formal calls soon opened her eyes to what she must expect from her new home. The European town, built at a fair distance from the native quarter, along the coastal road and overlooking the harbour, resembled strangely some mediocre townlet of the French provinces. Its architecture and conception were purely French and its mentality was that of the most backward province, with its scandal, mud-slinging and intrigue, multiplied a hundred-fold by political conditions and the Oriental genius for back-biting. The little town was divided into two venomously hostile clans, that of the mayor and that of his assistant, which spent the greater part of their time hurling mutual accusations of every conceivable crime and vice. Isolated from all contact with other Europeans, imprisoned in this narrow tongue of land that baked in torrid sun or seethed in mud according to the season, the slightest quarrels festered and swelled into murderous hatreds.

The Administration was the main centre of intrigue. Tenes was a 'mixed' municipality, administered by a council composed in equal parts of Arabs of French nationality and French functionaries, who, although civilians, wore uniforms and took military rank. The chief preoccupation of the European administrators was to maintain prestige and their own advantages in face of the native population and to crush any sign of originality among their own members. Each new arrival was forced, almost from the first day, to choose between the opposing parties and take part in the quarrelling and calumnies which were the only distraction available for the Europeans.

Isabelle was initiated without delay and called upon to make her choice between the rivals. She was the least aggressive of mortals and quite incapable of carrying on an intrigue or understanding the interest to be found in doing so, so she preferred to call in at the grocer's shop—which sold a little of everything, in the style of the village shops in Europe—buy a halfpenny note-book and a bottle of ink, and transpose the history of her arrival into a short story.

A young Frenchman, Bernard, arrives in a little town in Algeria to invest his small fortune in a farm. He enters the first of the two local inns where he is welcomed by a number of his compatriots:

' "So you've just arrived? One can see that . . . but as we're all Frenchmen here we can get things straight. . . . We know that *they* will try to get hold of you—the assistant mayor's lot. Look out for them . . . they're a set of rogues . . . no patriotic feeling. They are the ones who are ruining the colony. Can you imagine that at the senatorial elections they voted for Thingammy, the chap who is for the natives against the colonists. We are for the mayor, so don't let them get round you."

' "But I have not come to have anything to do with politics. I don't bother about all that. I just want to look around and work."

'The colonists gazed at him with an air of hostile surprise.

' "Oh, I know your sort! The Government gives concessions to all sorts of people from France who don't give a damn for the interests of the colony and won't back up the colonists, then our sons have to work like labourers with all those lousy rascals."

'And the colonist walked out.'

★　　　★　　　★

'The road was dark and deserted and after a walk, Bernard entered another inn. There too, people were shouting and arguing.

'Bernard joined a little group, quieter than the others, who were playing cards in a corner.

' "Well, gentlemen, how do things go out here? I have come out to be a colonist, like yourselves."

'At once Bernard noticed a certain embarrassment in the attitude of the card-players.

' "Where are you staying?"

' "In the first inn on the right, on the road to——"

'The card-players exchanged glances, as if he had said something abominable.

' "Hell! So that's how they recruit their lot now! But don't you know where you are there? The lot who go there are thieves, bandits. That's where the mayor's crowd meet. . . ."

' "But, I don't care. I'm only stopping there until I can build my own place."

' "You don't understand. You will be dishonoured if you stay with that lot. And then, they'll get hold of you. One can see you don't know the mayor."

'Once more Bernard tried to affirm his political independence, but he was interrupted.

"It is absolutely inadmissible. Here we believe in keeping the situation clear: one is with the honest chaps or with the thieves. It's no good arguing; that's how it is. . . ." '

The story would earn her a few shillings from Victor Barrucand, but the reality had to be faced. If Isabelle had suffered in Algiers from the narrow conventionality of the French and the degeneracy of the semi-occidentalized Arabs, she was to find the situation here a hundred times worse. In this little town, where a couple of thousand bored and spiteful Europeans had more or less exhausted each other as a subject for gossip, her every movement would be spied on and commentated. A European married to an Arab—and a mere ex-sergeant at that—figured as a traitor to the community; a writer was a dangerously eccentric person; and a woman of uncertain nationality who was manifestly unconcerned with the interests of the colony, must certainly be an agent for some unspecified but menacing political interest.

In the midst of this hot-bed of spying and rancour, there lived two men of quite different quality. One was Robert Arnaud, better known by his pen-name of Robert Randau, a cultured and truculent Frenchman, Africanist and Islamist of distinction and the ex-companion of the explorer Coppolani who had died at the hands of an assassin in Senegal. He had recently arrived with his wife from Timbuctoo, to take up the function of third adjutant in the Administration, exchanging with a colleague who had been put to flight by the quasi-necessity of taking sides in the local quarrels. Randau was a talented writer, with an individual style, who had already published a number of articles and a novel based on the life of the North African Jewish community, written in collaboration with Saadia Levy. He believed in the possibility of a characteristic North African school of literature and raged against the sugary and sentimental productions of the local writers who wrote pretty sketches of Arab life and of visiting men of letters who pontificated in the sole light of their own ignorance.

Randau, like most Algerian Frenchmen, knew Isabelle by name since the famous trial at Constantine and, intrigued by her story, had taken the trouble to question M. Luciani, the director of the Department of Native Affairs, on her subject. Luciani had replied that she was an adventuress whose case presented no interest, but Randau was not convinced and was delighted at the opportunity to satisfy his curiosity. Later he gave his own account of her arrival at Tenes:

'It was on 7th July 1902, that Isabelle and Sliman Ehnni arrived at Tenes by the diligence from Orleansville. . . . On the 8th, at about ten in the morning, two strangers in native costume had themselves announced. I received them in the narrow office (or rather, passage) in which, by virtue of my functions as an officer of the judicial police, I was presiding over a noisy confrontation between a cattle thief and several shepherds. One of the arrivals, who was very dark and appeared to be in ill-health, wore a moustache and had regular features and a pleasing face. He presented himself: Si Sliman Ehnni, the new *khodja* of the mixed municipality. His companion, slim and elegant, clad in the *haik* of a horseman, with an immaculately white burnous and shod with the *mestr* of the Spahis, had black eyes of extraordinary brilliance, a colourless face, high cheek-bones and reddish hair. Beneath the turban, near the ears and around the pale lips, the skin had the yellow, transparent look of parchment. "May I introduce Si Mahmoud Saadi," said the dark visitor; "that is her pseudonym; in reality she is Madame Ehnni, my wife."

'I welcomed my guests warmly and we were soon deep in conversation. After a few minutes, Ehnni took his leave and went off to continue his round of official visits. Isabelle, who had been told about me by a colleague who had no love for me, knew that I had taken part in the first Coppolani expedition and that a novel of mine, written in collaboration with Saadia Levy, had appeared in Paris; my Algerian luggage also comprised a few small volumes of verse. She mentioned them politely; I asked in my turn after her work and projects; she enumerated them obligingly; she was engaged in several novels, volumes of impressions, essays, etc. . . . She spoke slowly, as if seeking her words, with a particularly disagreeable and monotonous nasal voice; she lit cigarette after cigarette and interspersed her conversation with oaths. She laughed often, showing all her teeth, but was not in the least exuberant; her characteristic gesture was to carry her cigarette to her lips with her right hand while the left remained resting on her knee. Her behaviour was dignified, even grave. I may add that she was completely lacking in sex appeal.'

When Isabelle left the office, she and Randau were firm friends and had decided to follow a common policy of refusing to take the slightest interest in local politics. Randau appreciated Isabelle's informal comradeship, encouraged her to write and understood the restless spirit that sent her roaming out, for days and nights together, far into the *bled* among the tribes of the Beni-Merzoug and Beni-Haousa and the mountains of the Chelha.

The friendship with Robert Randau and his wife was soon extended to include Raymond Marival, another writer who was acting at the time as magistrate in Tenes and who preferred the society of the Symbolist poets whose works crowded the shelves of his tiny office to that of his censorious neighbours. The three families soon arranged for themselves an agreeable existence, composed largely of violent discussions on philosophy and literature—in which Isabelle took a prominent part in spite of her remarkable ignorance on many aspects of these two subjects; of couscous parties, at which she surprised her friends by preparing the savoury mess with the skill of a good Algerian housewife; and of long excursions on horseback into the country and impromptu picnics among the pinewoods and olive groves of the wild and charming sites along the coast.

They were often joined by visitors from Algiers—artists and writers or journalists who believed, like Randau and Marival, in a colonial policy which would protect French interests without despoiling the natives and in the possibility of upholding French prestige without cutting themselves off from and despising the Moslem population. There were projects for starting a review to express their point of view; of collaboration in novels, plays. The painter Noiré, who spent his life roaming over all Algeria in search of subjects, often came to join their group, participated in the excursions and appreciated Isabelle as a comrade. The Leblond brothers sometimes came, bringing their prestige as successful Parisian men of letters, and a little way along the coast Elysée Reclus, who had lived in exile in Geneva during Isabelle's childhood and must have known Trophimovsky and the household at the Villa Neuve, had founded an anarchist colony.

Robert Randau has evoked in his souvenirs of Isabelle's life in Tenes, a curious episode that took place on one of these picnics. With Marival, several friends from the neighbourhood and a number of *fellaheen* as guides, they had ridden out to a wild valley, whose hollow was filled with exotic trees and aromatic plants and where a waterfall thundered down through rocky chasms, so that the place was cool and dim as a house of marble. Isabelle and Marival argued noisily, as usual; the women of the party prepared a meal which was eaten amid boisterous good humour; the *fellaheen*, who had discovered a forgotten bottle of rum, began the preparations for the return journey in a state of noisy exaltation.

Isabelle was mounted on Ziza, Randau's little white mare, with whom she had fallen in love at first sight and which she came to consider almost as her own property. The caravan was on the way home and passing through a desolate stretch of common, overgrown with scrub, thorny bushes and thistles, when her curiosity was aroused by a ruined hut, half-hidden in a thicket, its roof of woven rushes unravelled and flapping in the breeze.

Isabelle exclaimed at the strange, deserted aspect of this miserable place and added: 'I can't explain why or how, but it seems to me as though the hut is breathing.'

A moment later she had dropped on hands and knees, crawled into the interior, and her companions heard her striking a match.

An instant later there came a cry: 'Come quickly, Arnaud. There's a poor devil here who is just going to pass out!'

In the dark and stinking hut an old Arab, incredibly thin and shivering with cold, lay stretched on the floor of beaten mud, beneath a sort of curtain of cobwebs that festooned the walls. He had a long white beard, his head reposed on a rusty sieve and his body was crawling with vermin. Isabelle questioned him gently as to the reason for his abandonment and he answered her in a quavering old voice, interrupted by bursts of cavernous coughing:

'Up to the end I was able to guard the cattle in the fields with my children's children. When I became too weak even for that, my sons carried me to this hut and it is here that the angels of death will come to fetch me. The harvest has been bad. There are barely enough barley cakes for the workers and their children; I am no longer able to work and I have not the right to eat the pittance of those who labour. My sons gave me a dish of cooked beans and a jar of water. Each evening, one of my grandchildren knocks at the door of the hut with his stick and cries: "Old man, are you dead?" And I reply: "No." Then he goes away. When I have eaten all my beans, I shall die. The child who calls to me will hear no answer. He will tell his parents and they will bury me as befits a Moslem. Everything conforms to the will of God.'

For all Isabelle's resignation to Fate and belief in the fore-written destiny of man, this was too much for her. The European in her revolted against the cruelty of these children and the blind acceptance of the father. Sobbing with indignation and pity, she declared that the old man must be saved, that the children must be forced to provide for him, that he must be removed at once from this horrible den.

'Justice', whispered the old man, 'belongs only to Allah, and retribution is his alone. Nothing happens in this world except by his will and I am resigned to it.'

Isabelle could not make up her mind to leave him to his fate and, with the aid of Arnaud and a couple of the *fellaheen*, he was carried out of the hut and laid on such coverings as could be provided while she fed him gently with grapes and figs; then when he was a little restored, she had him placed on the back of one of the mules and led slowly to the town.

When they reached Tenes, she supervised his installation at the hospital, gave him money to pay for the best treatment that could be had and began without delay her search for the unfilial sons—a difficult task, since the old man refused to give their name or his own or to betray their dwelling-place.

But when morning came, the old Arab had disappeared. He had used the money to hire a mule and had ridden off in the darkness to some wild place where he could die according to the desire of his children and the evident will of God.

This short tragedy moved Isabelle deeply, and she hardly knew whether to admire and envy the perfect faith and submission of this simple and ignorant peasant or whether to react in horror against the conditions which reduced a family to such a pitch of misery that its 'useless mouths' must be left to starve so that the young might continue to labour. More and more she came to identify herself with her brother-Moslems and especially with the poor and dispossessed, those whom Brieux had urged her to help and in whose cause Barrucand encouraged her to intervene.

Barrucand's influence was, at this period, the most important element in her life. The new journal, *Akhbar*—'The News' —was ready to appear and he intended to make it the organ of his own opinions, extend its circulation among the native population and thereby gain an important political foothold among the Arabs. Isabelle was to supply a regular column, consisting of sketches of native life and the customs of the Bedouin tribes with whom she was on terms of easy familiarity and among whom her Qadrya chaplet served as an invaluable passport.

The assignment suited her perfectly, since it provided an excuse for escaping from the stifling atmosphere of Tenes, where the sneers and calumnies were mounting against her, into the nomad life of the surrounding *bled*. The long rides into the solitude of the mountains calmed her exacerbated nerves and the contact with the simple unspoiled people of the interior washed away the horrid souvenir of the mayor, his assistant and all the 'band of pretentious Philistines who imagine they are important because they wear tight trousers, a ridiculous hat or a *képi* with the insignia of an officer.' If the terrible experiences of the last two years had made it possible for Isabelle to appreciate the relative security of her new life and, above all, the home shared at last with 'Zuizou', they had not tamed her restless temperament. When Arnaud, half-curious and half-teasing, professed his astonishment at her frequent absences and Sliman's patient acceptance of them, she protested that her husband knew very well that her heart remained with him, but that she could not do otherwise than follow her destiny. Arnaud, pursuing his idea, inquired indiscreetly what she would do if ever she had a child.

'All Russian woman', she replied with dignity, 'are excellent mothers and I should be as good as any of them. Only, if I had a child I should not give up my wanderings but I should carry him with me, strapped to my saddle, wherever I went.' But she added that she had no wish to become a mother.

Often she would ride out to the Main, to Baghdoura, Tarzout, to Cap Kalax or to M'gueu. Sometimes she would lodge in the house of the *caïd* or sometimes content herself with the humble hospitality of the Moorish café, where any traveller, man or woman, could sleep unmolested, his or her safety guaranteed by the immemorial tradition of Islam. She frequented the marabouts, discussed theology with them and heard rumours of the revolt that grumbled in the South and the trouble along the Moroccan border. She listened to the complaints of the farmers—victims of the insatiable rapacity of the Mayor of Tenes, who combined usury with his official functions; she noted the plight of the ex-Spahis, who, their period of military service ended, could no longer adapt themselves to the primitive and patriarchal life of the tribes; she talked to the women, filthy beneath their gaudy rags, who lived in crumbling huts on the outskirts of the villages and sold themselves to passing soldiers or the unmarried boys who suffered in the long, hot nights. She encouraged people of every sort to confide in her, which they did readily, since they found in her the comradeship that was usually only possible between men, together with the sympathy and intuition of a woman and the learning and wise counsel of a sage.

Once, on the deserted road between Boghari and Laghouat, she came on a column of prisoners, wending their way up to the penitentiary of Taadmith, hidden among the icy peaks of the high tableland. They were chained together, bare-footed and forced by their guards to walk along the ridge of sharp stones that formed the middle of the road. They had never been judged by any regular court, but had been condemned without possibility of appeal by European administrators or the denunciation of some local *caïd* to years of lonely suffering in the terrible prisons where they would rot slowly, with no hope of mercy and no one to whom they might look for help.

'It was like a vision in an evil dream', she noted.

She was a tireless journalist now. Whenever a fête was held in some distant village, Isabelle was there, sketching the scene in the simple hardy phrases that Barrucand would have liked to, and sometimes did, polish into his idea of a literary gem. Whenever some flagrant injustice of the Administration was signalled, she arrived—by mule, on horseback or on foot—to make her inquiries. *Akhbar* had been founded to champion the native cause, but it could not, in the present state of colonization, go too far or risk outraging the feelings of the Administration. There were long discussions as to what could and could not be printed. Often Barrucand sent for her to come to Algiers and then she bade good-bye to Sliman and set off, delighted to spend a few weeks far from the poisoned atmosphere of Tenes. Then, comfortably installed in the charming villa, she began to regret the poverty-stricken home and the presence that was the only thing that really bound her to life. Sliman's health gave her great anxiety and the constant vexations to which he was subjected in his quality of *khodja* were too much for his failing strength. If only, thought Isabelle, he could be appointed *caïd* of some distant village, far out in the *bled*, away from the corruption of the semi-occidentalized coastal region; if only they could return to the South, to the Souff with its pure dry climate and the austere probity of its customs. Then, despairing of the French colonies, she dreamed for a moment of Palestine, of settling in Nablus, among a nobler sort of Arab and near the holy city of Jerusalem. . . . Anywhere to escape from the 'imbecile Europeans who poison the country with their presence . . . indiscreet, arrogant beings who imagine they have the right to bring everything down to the same level, to make everything resemble their own ugly effigy'. Thus wrote Isabelle in a moment of discouragement, weakened by one of the attacks of malarial fever that were gradually undermining her once solid health.

In Algiers, the affairs of *Les Nouvelles* and *Akhbar* kept her continually occupied. She was Barrucand's chief collaborator, and besides her regular articles she was acting as general adviser on native questions and helping with publicity and sales. Her striking appearance, her romantic history and the mystery that surrounded her origin, sometimes attracted more attention than she cared for. At a Press banquet, given in April 1903 in honour of President Loubet, who was then on an official visit to Algiers, the representative of an important French provincial newspaper noticed the strange figure of the young Arab seated near Barrucand and inquired from his neighbours who he might be. The information was willingly given, with details that were sometimes true and sometimes false, but always set out in the most unfavourable light. The result was an article in *La Petite Gironde*, in which outright accusations and subtle insinuations combined to make a sensational story:

'A lady assisted at the banquet offered last night by the Association of Algerian Journalists to the foreign Press. She was a colleague.

'Madame Henni, *née* Isabelle Eberhardt, writes for the journal *Akhbar*. She has a history. Arriving in Algeria with her mother, some years ago, the latter died a short while later, leaving her alone. She then embraced the Moslem religion and went to live in the Southern Territories, where she soon became an ardent propagandist among the Arabs, preaching to them a sort of humanitarian Socialism that did not conceal her animosity against France.

'Isabelle Eberhardt is of Russian origin. She is supposed to possess a considerable fortune. What is certain is that she exercised in the South certain liberalities which rendered her propaganda yet more dangerous. The authorities took steps at last and issued a mandate of expulsion against her, but, at this moment Isabelle declared that she was on the point of marrying a native who was a naturalized French citizen. The marriage did, in fact, take place soon after and Miss Isabelle, now Madame Henni, and a Frenchwoman into the bargain, escaped the effects of the mandate.

'The modification of her status, far from putting a stop to her sermons, gave her fresh wind, and now she not only preached, but wrote. Her prestige among the natives grew from day to day; the Arabs consider her as a marabout. Her case is all the more surprising when one thinks of their scorn of women, who remain for them creatures of no importance.

'As a matter of fact, she has abandoned the clothes of her sex. Still better, she has renounced European costume and deliberately adopted the tarbush, which encircles the head, and the *haik*, which falls from the crown and envelops the body without a fold; the gandourah and boots of morocco leather. The transformation is thus complete.

'It was in this guise that we saw her at the banquet last night. She is young; her physiognomy is most agreeable, her voice is soft and musical. She talks simply and with great charm, but it would appear that she is quite different when she is engaged in evangelizing in Arabic. Then she takes on the angry accents and violent images of the Prophets. It seems that she represents the French as being the best friends of the Jews and, as the Arabs detest the Jews above all else, one may imagine the dangers of assimilation,[1] as cleverly exploited by the pythoness. Madame Henni's husband is an interpreter in the South, where he continues to reside.'

This was the first article that ever appeared on Isabelle in the French Press. One of the incongruous elements in Isabelle's character was that she was far from adverse to publicity and the annoyance caused by the unpleasant tone of the article was partly compensated for since it gave her the opportunity of refuting it in a long letter in which she presented herself as she wished to appear before the public. In it she protested her innocence, her affection for France and mocked at the idea that she had any political or religious influence among the tribes. She also added a few details of her own invention, insisting notably that she was a Moslem by birth. *La Petite Gironde* published her letter, but the curiosity aroused by the controversy soon died down.

---

[1] The Jews, in French North Africa, were automatically assimilated—that is, considered as French citizens—whereas the Arabs had to qualify for naturalization.

Chapter Fourteen

T HE most difficult of all things—the only difficult thing perhaps,' wrote Isabelle in her diary, on Christmas Day, 1902, 'is to enfranchise oneself and —even harder—to live in freedom. Anyone who is in the least free is the enemy of the mob, to be systematically persecuted, tracked down wherever he takes refuge. I am becoming more and more irritated against this life and the people who refuse to allow any exception to exist and who accept their own slavery and try to impose it on others.'

It was towards the end of the month-long fast of Ramadan. Like all her fellow-Moslems, she had abstained, during the whole month, from eating, drinking or smoking between dawn and dusk. Like all the rest of the millions of followers of Islam throughout the world, she had scanned the sky anxiously each evening, with a clamouring stomach and tense nerves, waiting for the moment 'when a man can no longer distinguish a white thread from a black' at which it would be lawful to satisfy the needs of the body. Ordinarily she loved this season, when the privation of the body seemed to liberate the spirit, to encourage meditation and dreaming, but this year it was impossible to abstract her thoughts from the thousand petty troubles that invaded her life at every instant.

This woman who shrank from the contact of all but the poorest and most humble, who asked for nothing—neither for comfort nor money nor for any kind of material advantage, but only to be left in peace to follow the law of her own nature—seemed to sow enemies like dragons' teeth wherever she passed. At El Oued and at Batna, she had been reviled and traduced as an adventuress, a spy and a debauchee. She had defended herself as well as she could by a series of letters to the Press, but her instinct was to shrink away from the calumny and despise the calumnators, rather than to go out to meet them. Here in Tenes, where gossip and spite were the chief recreations and where she could make no move without being observed, her essential difference took on the proportions of a crime.

It was, above all, her long and frequent disappearances that gave rise to so much ill-disposed speculation. Where did she go? What did she do? What were her relations with the wild semi-nomad people of the Ouarsenis mountains and their desert hinterland? These were the mysteries that were discussed at length in many prim French homes and not a few Arab ones, and the most extravagant suppositions were soon being passed on as proved facts.

In reality, Isabelle's escapades, besides their professional *raison d'être*, were largely a seeking for escape. The cultivated fields and neat plantations of Tenes exacerbated her nerves almost as much as did the society of the little town. One night, stretched out on the rush matting of some Moorish café far out in the Main or in the mountain country, she scribbled some notes in pencil:

'There are few intellectuals' she wrote, 'who care to claim their right to the life of a wanderer, to *vagabondage*.

'Yet vagabondage means escape from slavery and the life of the roads means liberty.

'To take the decision, to cast off all the bonds with which

modern life and the weakness of our own hearts have charged us, to arm ourselves with the symbolic sack and staff of the pilgrim and *to depart*. . . .

'For anyone who understands the value and also the exquisite flavour of solitary freedom (for one is only really free when one is alone) the act of departure is the bravest and most beautiful of all.

'A selfish happiness perhaps. But it is happiness, for him who knows how to appreciate it.

'To be alone, to have no needs, to be unknown, a stranger and at home everywhere, and to march, solitary and great, to the conquest of the world. . . .'

Then the memory of the constant injustice and persecution she had suffered swept over her, disturbing and soiling her ardent dream of liberty:

'The pariah in our modern society', she continued, 'is the nomad and vagabond, "without any fixed abode".

'When the men of law and order add these words to the name of someone in an irregular situation, they believe they have stigmatized him for ever.

'To possess a home, a family, property or some sort of public function, to have some definite means of existence, in fact, to be a cog in the social machine—these are the things that seem necessary and indispensable to the great majority of men, even to intellectuals and to those who believe themselves to be enfranchised.

'Yet all that is only a variety of the slavery into which we are dragged by the contact with our fellows, and, above all, by a contact that is regulated and continual. . . .

'Not to feel the torturing need to know and see what lies out there, beyond the mysterious blue walls of the horizon. . . . Not to be oppressed by the depressing monotony of the same landscape. . . . To watch the road that leads away into the unknown distance without feeling the imperative need to give oneself up to it, to follow it docilely over mountains and valleys. . . . All this timid liking for immobility resembles the unconscious resignation of the animal, drugged by servitude, that holds out its neck towards the harness.

'All property has its bounds and all power is subject to some law, but the tramp possesses the whole vast earth, whose only limits are the unreal horizon and his empire is intangible since he governs it and enjoys it in the spirit.'

In the simple tribal society of these almost untouched regions, Isabelle found something of the peace and dignity of the Souff. Everyone knew that she was a woman, but she was always greeted by her Arab title of Si Mahmoud and no villager would have been discourteous enough to betray that her real identity was no secret to him. Everywhere she passed, there was some problem waiting to be submitted to her, for she was a person of learning, a *m'sakofi*, with a smattering of medicine and of law besides a Koranic science that was not often equalled in these regions where the djinns and spirits of the old pagan days still haunted the imagination of an untutored and superstitious people. There would be a dispute over the ownership of some plot of land, or a sick baby would have refused to respond to the traditional treatment by charms and dried cattle-dung, or a couple of elders would be in disagreement as to the interpretation of some verse of the Koran. Isabelle, arriving on horseback—generally on Ziza, whom she had almost adopted as her own—would be taken off to the café and there, sitting cross-legged among the men of the village, she would listen gravely to their troubles, draw them out to talk, to confide in her their intimate problems and reveal the curious customs whose roots were buried in an uncharted past and which had been guarded jealously from the knowledge of Europeans. The night would wear by in drowsy talk over the *kif* pipes and the coffee cups and in the morning Isabelle would have enriched her tribal lore with new knowledge, new legends.

Yet there was danger in these nights, for Isabelle never realized that in the eyes of many of the austere Moslems in these regions untouched by the corruption of the towns, she was a heretic. Abdallah had repeated obstinately to the court in Constantine: 'She brings disorder into our religion', and for certain fanatics her masculine dress and her unconcealed fondness for *aguardiente*—the potent Spanish anisette liquor—were as disconcerting as her conversation. The convert to Islam remained indeed more European than she ever suspected. Though her integration into Arab life was perhaps more complete than that of any *roumia* before her, her mind had been formed in the logical tradition of the West. When she spoke of charity, she meant the active charity of the Christian philosophy she had rejected, and the tortuous paths of intrigue, which are the essence of Arab mentality and whose absence is in itself suspicious, were absolutely foreign to her. So she made enemies among those she considered as her own people, simply by being herself. She was spied on in the mountains and the desert as she was in the town and, if ninety-nine villagers blessed her name for the help she brought to the sick and the advice she gave to the unlettered, there was always one hostile listener to note her slightest remark and carry it back, distorted and potentially dangerous, to her enemies.

Back in Tenes, a certain important member of the Mayor's clan listened hungrily to the evil rumours concerning her and took care to spread them as far afield as possible. He was an unpleasant person who had already been in trouble with the law for various nefarious financial deals with the natives, had been forced to resign a previous post and held his present position only through political protection. He was a great amateur of women and he had made it a point of honour to add Isabelle to his collection. She had repulsed him with more than her usual crudity of language and he had gone off swearing vengeance. From that time on he never lost an opportunity of propagating stories of her supposed debauchery during those long absences which Sliman supported with such curious equanimity.

When Randau warned her of danger, Isabelle refused to take the threat seriously and continued to give her own version of the affair amid peals of laughter at the memory of the gallant functionary's discomfiture. Yet her friends could see that she was becoming more and more feverish and unstable in this hostile atmosphere. Sometimes she drank to drown her growing despair and then, under the influence of the terrible *aguardiente*, rode out madly into the night or threw herself down on the ground, in a paroxysm of misery to weep and moan for hours at a time. Sometimes she would return at dawn, exhausted and dishevelled, often shivering with malarial fever, and take refuge with Arnaud and his wife, who did the best they could to comfort her. Once, after a terrible scene with Sliman—occasioned by the inevitable difference in their conception of love—he and Isabelle decided to kill themselves and set out, armed with revolver and bottles of anisette, to a distant spot where they were to accomplish the deed. But Sliman was so moved by the beauty of the night and the grandeur of the death that awaited him, that he began to recite interminable poems on the beauty of love and death. Isabelle riposted with more verses and as the moon grew higher the contents of the bottles grew lower. They awoke long after dawn, drenched, shivering and ashamed, but with no more desire to kill themselves, and returned on foot through a town agog with interest.

Such eccentricities did not escape the watchful eyes of the 'Mayor's clan', nor did the disorder of Isabelle's finances. She might have been able to live in modest security with Sliman's salary as *khodja*—although a thousand francs a year would not go far even in those days—and the small payments she received from Barrucand if she had been a careful, calculating house-wife. But she was incorrigibly negligent. Any money she possessed was spent immediately on tobacco, on books, on gifts to any native who came to her with a story of illness or of exploitation by the colonists. Often she discovered at the last minute that she had not enough to buy food, and then she would slip round to the Jewish quarter and seek out the bearded pawnbroker, sitting among the extraordinary collection of junk accumulated from indigent natives. Sliman's extra burnous or a stick of furniture from the now almost denuded home would provide, after much bargaining, a sum sufficient for some dates, a few cigarettes and a handful of couscous. Or, if there was nothing to pawn, she would address a little note to Randau, begging his help:

'Dear friend,
'As I have nothing to make a meal, I want to ask you, if you can manage it, to lend me five francs to live on for a few days.
'If you can do this, will you send me the stuff directly by my little messenger, so there shall not be any gossip. Thank you in advance. . . .'

'Dear comrade,
'I am going to bore you again by asking you another favour.
'I shall be here till the beginning of August and I have absolutely nothing to eat. Lend me ten francs if you can and I will give something to the baker and buy a little meat, which I have not tasted for a long time.
'Try to do this for poor Mahmoud who looks like living up to his name before long.
'Among other good news, I have received a summons from one of my creditors. Mektoub!'

In spite of the brave attempt she made to hide this state of affairs from the eyes of the neighbours, her misadventures were soon the subject of hostile gossip through the whole of Tenes, where what she bitterly described as a 'troop of females —neurotic, orgiastic, senseless and cruel', watched greedily for the weak point in her defences. Her habit of pawning her belongings soon became common knowledge, and on April Fool's Day of that year some of them found it amusing to send her an imitation of a pawn-ticket for 'one straw mattress'. Isabelle kept the horrid little piece of paper as a sort of bitter souvenir and it was found among her letters and manuscripts after her death.

Both Randau and Marival had occasional glimpses of Isabelle's utter distress of mind at this period, but neither of them understood its essential cause. Both were Frenchmen of the Rabelaisian tradition—convivial, curious of life, attracted to the ironical, the grotesque and the picturesque. Both appreciated Isabelle as a good comrade and admired her intellectual qualities. They were broad-minded enough to understand that her eccentricities and the way of life which in a creature less talented might have seemed sordid, were essential aspects of a nature which, as a whole, they loved and admired. They saw in her the talented hoyden, the amazon with an astonishing knowledge of nomad life, the bizarre artist who must be cajoled out of fits of melancholy, but the insatiable mystic of the diaries was never revealed to them.

Raymond Marival, the lively little novelist-magistrate with his ready jokes, his erudition and the Provençal accent that was the joy of Isabelle and Randau, commemorated, after her death, one of these fits of despair which both he and Randau attributed to the insults and cruel mockeries of the town:

'Behind the house in which I lived at this period was a garden enclosed by a fence; a vine, a wild fig tree and a few flowering rose bushes were its only ornament. The noise of the town did not reach it and one could hear nothing but the confused murmur of the sea and of the great sea-gulls that circled in the air with piercing cries.

'Isabelle loved this retreat and used to come there almost every evening. She would sit on a bench, legs crossed and eyes vague, and silently smoke cigarettes of pale tobacco perfumed with musk. On the evening of which I speak, dusk had fallen and moths were fluttering around the lamp. Suddenly, in the shadow, I thought I heard a sob. Isabelle was crying, her elbows on her knees and her head in her hands.

' "What is the matter?" I asked. "What is the matter, Si Mahmoud?"

' She lifted her wet face reluctantly and fixed me with eyes full of distress, the eyes of a hunted animal. It lasted for only a second. As I approached, anxious at this breakdown, her face was covered again with the rather cold mask of careless serenity with which she usually faced her troubles.'

Marival and Randau took it for granted that Isabelle's distress was occasioned entirely by the campaign against her in the town. The yearning for the Absolute—the absolute union with the Unique Being which is the goal of Sufism—which she confided to her diary, escaped them completely. They were aware that she professed Islam and that she shared a good number of the astonishing collection of superstitions and half-pagan beliefs that distinguish the Berber population of Algeria from the austerer Moslems of the Middle East, but nothing in her behaviour led them to suspect that she aspired to advance on the path to Truth.

It was the impossibility of delivering herself from the contact of the world that threw Isabelle into despair—and perhaps also the impossibility of deliverance from herself and the terrible inheritance of the de Moerders.

'Ah, where is that far-off Thebia', she wrote in her diary. 'Where I shall escape at last from the imbecility of my fellow-creatures and where my senses will at last cease to trouble me?'

To retire into the desert, to live alone under the enormous sky in communion with the Infinite, to imitate those old Fathers of the Christian Church—such was Isabelle's impossible dream ... impossible because she would never be at peace with herself, because she would always be a slave to her senses and because all her efforts to escape from the human contacts that diminished the spiritual power she knew herself to possess, were frustrated by the ill-will and the incomprehension of her fellows.

The climax was rapidly approaching now. The Mayor was determined to get rid of his rivals and while eliminating them to neutralize the inconvenient rumours that were circulating on his own activities. The assistant mayor, M. Bouchet, leader of the rival clan, was supported by powerful political interests and it was not easy or safe to attack him directly. The imprudent Isabelle, on the other hand, was an easy prey and a resourceful *coup* against her would have the double advantage of satisfying a desire for personal revenge, and dealing an indirect and perhaps mortal blow at the principal enemy.

A visit from Barrucand provided the occasion. Isabelle, during her visits to Algiers, had described the life of Tenes with such drollery and malice that it had been easy to persuade him to spend a few days enjoying the situation for himself. As a self-conscious man of letters he was delighted at the opportunity for literary chats with Randau and Marival—both of them old acquaintances. Furthermore, he supported a certain candidate for the representation of the region who had a lively interest in the circumscription and counted on a wide circulation for *Akhbar* in native circles as a deciding factor in the forthcoming elections.

Barrucand, then, arrived in Tenes and was promptly introduced to Monsieur Bouchet. It was soon decided that the two of them, with Isabelle for guide, should make an excursion into the surrounding country, visit the principal cheikhs and combine a study of local conditions with a discreet campaign for stimulating the circulation of *Akhbar*.

The expedition lasted for several days and the trio were well received wherever they went. They visited the magnificent old cheikh whom the natives named Papa Hyena because of the extortionate taxes he wrung from even the poorest *fellah* in the region. He was of a noble line and had fought first against the French and then at their side against the rebel Kabyles. His keen intelligence, piety and striking appearance impressed Isabelle greatly and it was hard to make her believe —since she was nothing less than cynical—how well-founded was his evil reputation. . . . Then there were other notables, *caïds* and cheikhs who ruled over a handful of half-starved, resigned *fellahin*; marabouts who could neither read nor write but conversed in formulas of stately dignity. Everywhere they were received with the most courteous hospitality and her two companions noticed that Isabelle was treated with a respect that amounted almost to veneration.

Shortly after their return the scandal broke. Rumours had been spreading around the town, insidiously encouraged by her ex-suitor, that Isabelle's frequent absences had a political, and even a financial motive. The excursion provided a good excuse for the traducers to come into the open and bring a definite accusation. On 2nd April 1903, the *Union Républicaine*, devoted to the interests of the rival candidate and of the Mayor, issued a challenge in the form of two letters written by colonists in the region of Tenes. The second and most explicit ran:

'Sir,

'Kindly allow one of our colonist readers to give you a few details about the association Barrucand, Bouchet, Mahmoud and Co.

'A little while before the reappearance of the journal *Ahkbar*, M. Barrucand came to our region to discuss matters with his friend, the administrator, Bouchet. . . .

'This administrator, who usually avoids making the rounds, put himself out that day and took M. Barrucand to visit the tribes in his circumscription and introduced the sage of sages to his dependants.

'They were accompanied by Madame Mahmoud-Saadi Eberhardt and it was noticed that the administrator affected in front of the natives an extreme deference for the wife of his *khodja*, who was disguised as a male native.

'This reverent attitude went far beyond that which French courtesy requires towards a woman. Its aim was visibly to impress the onlookers with Madame Eberhardt's more or less official influence as a marabout. . . .

'The association Eberhardt, Barrucand, Bouchet, through the exploitation of the journal *Akhbar* which squeezes the natives dry on the pretext of defending their interests, probably pays well; in any case, it is ingenious.

'One can judge of it by the repartition of the rôles and the functions. M. Barrucand signs and edits his review. The administrator furnishes appropriate themes. Madame Eberhardt, dressed as a male Moslem, is enthroned in the office of her husband, *khodja* of the mixed community of Tenes, and holds mysterious conversations with all the natives as they come in and out of the offices.

'Furthermore, Madame Eberhardt makes equally mysterious rounds of the *douars*, mounted on the horse of the assistant Administrator and escorted by native policemen.

'We have decided to throw light on the game of this new Holy Trinity and we shall take measures.

'For a group of colonists,

'OTTO MOBYL.'

Almost at the same time an accusation of extortion, supported by a number of witnesses, was brought against Sliman.

M. Bouchet, an irritable and obstinate man, knew himself to be irrevocably implicated in the affair and fought with every means in his power against the machinations of his hated rival. Unfortunately he had a number of things to hide. The situation became more and more inextricably tangled. The witnesses against Sliman were proved to have been paid or intimidated; counter-accusations against the Mayor revealed a number of transactions which should normally have brought him to prison. Politicians intervened, the Press shrieked wholesale accusations of corruption. Isabelle wrote open letters pointing out that it was ridiculous to accuse her of trying to play the rôle of a prophetess and a marabout among the tribes and that she had more than once given the proof of her loyalty to the French. Finally nothing was proved against anyone but mud stuck to all concerned. The Mayor was forced to resign, the assistant mayor took another post, and Sliman, giving in his own resignation, was appointed as *khodja* in Guégour.

Chapter Fifteen

THE visit of President Loubet to Algiers had serious motives, for the year 1903 was destined to be one of the most eventful in the history of the colony. The long-discussed expedition to the Moroccan frontier, which Isabelle had foreseen three years earlier, could no longer be postponed. Ain-Sefra, which marked the southernmost point of the French penetration of the Sahara in the department of Oran, had become a death-trap and, under the terms of the agreement with the Sultan of Morocco, it was impossible to keep order in the region.[1] The new Sultan, the weak and frivolous Abd-ul-Aziz, had no shadow of authority over the frontier tribes on his side of the border and the real chief in that land was a dissident Algerian cheikh named Bou-Amama, a fanatic under whose influence razzias, murder and pillage flourished increasingly. His bands of warlike Beni-Guil would descend into Algeria, terrorize the tribes, assassinate the French, plunder all they could find and escape over the

[1] The Franco-Moroccan Agreement of 1845 stipulated that 'the territorial limits between the two countries are not to be established, since the ground cannot be cultivated and serves as pasture land for the Arabs of the two Empires, who carry these for water and pasturage'.

border where the sparse troops of the region had not the right to pursue them. When the new Governor-General, M. Jonnart, arrived that year to take up his post, he was greeted on his first day of office by the news of several murders and of the capture of an important food-convoy, and when he himself imprudently ventured into the region of Ain-Sefra, his convoy was attacked and he came within an inch of being kidnapped.

This Monsieur Jonnart was an energetic and intelligent man who had drawn his conclusions from the events at Margueritte and had little patience with the timid policy of the authorities in Paris. He understood the impossibility of negotiating with a Sultan who took more interest in electric toys imported from Europe than in the affairs of government, whose wives preened themselves in silk dresses and plumed hats and whose conduct had long ago cost him the respect of the primitive and intransigent Moslems of his barbaric kingdom. On the other hand, information from agents in the country suggested that the Moroccans themselves were tired of anarchy, revolted by the ceaseless extortions of the marauding tribes and would regard foreign intervention with a favourable eye. France seemed indicated for the rôle of tutor, but Spain and Germany were watching jealously and England regarded with suspicion the growing colonial power of her principal rival. M. Jonnart found himself faced with the subtle problem of putting an end to an intolerable state of affairs in the frontier region without arousing the hostility of the Sultan or the jealousy of European neighbours. Troop movements, in view of the political situation, had to be cautious and gradual.

However, on August 17th, the French outpost at Taghit had been attacked by four thousand of Bou-Amama's *djiouch* and Isabelle's old acquaintance, Captain de Susbielle, had been hard put to it to save his garrison. Then, a few days later, there had been a veritable battle near El-Moungar, where a convoy had halted imprudently in the valley and fallen victim to the bandits, leaving thirty-six dead and forty-seven wounded.

The sub-division of Ain-Sefra was in a state of undeclared warfare.

The eyes of all Europe were fixed by now on this distant corner of the Sahara and correspondents from the French Press were arriving daily and installing themselves, not without repugnance, in such primitive accommodation as the region could offer. The Algerian papers too, sent their representatives and it was thus that Barrucand proposed that Isabelle should follow the troops as reporter for *Akhbar*.

She had passed painful months in Algiers, still crushed by the sordid experiences of Tenes, pursued by an ignominious Press campaign which saw in her a useful pawn in an especially base political campaign and a woman who, since she was no longer covered by the conventional protection of society, could be jeered at and reviled with impunity. For the first time her stubborn belief in the fraternity of man was shaken. She could no longer, she complained, tell her friends from her enemies. Misfortune and ill-health had reduced her temporarily to a state of stupefaction, 'without joy or sorrow', and it was from this semi-dream that she was awaked by the sudden prospect of a marvellous departure.

Several days of exhausting travel brought her to Ain Sefra, 'somnolent and Saharian', crouched at the foot of the towering Plateaux and facing the limitless desert. The little town was stirring with unusual animation. There was a coming and going of troops, of Spahis, *Mokhaznis* mounted on their skinny little horses, native soldiers of all kinds, in their gay cloaks and embroidered burnous. They filled the Moorish cafés, the improvised canteen and the covered passages of beaten sand that formed the streets of the townlet, with their plaintive music and harsh cries. There were young French officers, a little stiff and conscious of their dignity, followed at every step by swarms of children who had learned the whole art of begging since the arrival of the Army. There were men of the Foreign Legion—blond giants from the North, strayed to the desert through crime or disappointment or simply the nostalgia of the unknown; or ex-soldiers of

Garibaldi who had followed their chief to France and, exiled, engaged in the Legion after his death.

The hospital was filled with the wounded from El-Moungar and Isabelle's first article in *Akhbar* consisted in a series of interviews with the Legionaries who recounted, from their beds in the overcrowded ward, the epic of that fateful day; the careless jokes of the imprudent Captain Vauchez, who had sworn to ride to Tafilalet 'in his shirt-sleeves' and had died in the valley, spending his last strength in scribbling the note that would warn de Susbielle of the catastrophe and bring him to the rescue of the little band of survivors; the gallant death of the Danish officer Selkhausen; the terrible thirst that had tortured the men all through that day, since they had been surprised waterless and unprepared. In another ward were the native *goumiers*, primitive men who lived for fighting and considered all the imposing military preparations as mere counter-razzias, reprisals for tribal raids, normal in this troubled region which they called among themselves *bled-el-baroud*, the powder country. Most of them were *zouas*, half-bred Berbers, crossed with Arab, undersized but wiry. They were furnished by the local tribes as a sort of feudal tribute to the French masters and served under French officers as scouts and guides.

It was among such men that Isabelle lived by preference, sharing their simple life as far as regulations permitted and respected by these illiterate Bedouin as one whose learning permitted him the ineffable honour of reading the Koran. She lodged in the Arab *fondouks* or slept on the floors of Moorish cafés and followed when she could obtain permission—and sometimes by fraud—reconnoitres to outlying villages. Then she slept with the *goumiers* in the stifling shelter of their tents, shared with them their meals of dates and couscous, participated in their privations and fatigues. 'I live the desert life', she wrote, 'as simply as the camel-drivers and the *mokhazni*.'

Yet, if she lived by choice among the native troops who knew her only as poor Mahmoud Saadi, ravaged by malaria and worn by starvation, certain officers were aware of her identity and intrigued by her personality. On the whole, though with certain notable exceptions, she had always received more comprehension from the military than from civilians, and now, at this time of common exaltation and in the excitement of approaching battle, several of these officers became her comrades and even her lasting friends. One of them undertook to introduce her to the new Commander of the sub-division, who had arrived to take up his post almost at the same time as herself and who was to play an important and indeed decisive rôle in her life.

The appointment of Lyautey, who was still a colonel at the time of his arrival, had been secured by the astute M. Jonnart after some difficult negotiations with the Foreign Office in Paris. His figure already dominated Ain-Sefra as it was soon to dominate all North Africa. He had been Chief-of-Staff to the great General Galliéni in Indo-China and administrator of a vast territory in Madagascar under the same chief. He was an intellectual as well as a great soldier. His subordinates, whom he treated as collaborators, adored him and the Arabs appreciated his fine horsemanship, his elegance and the qualities of a *grand seigneur* which he displayed freely and which his enemies stigmatized as showing off. He was a remarkable judge of men and allowed neither prejudice nor officialdom to stand in his way or prevent him using each of his officers according to the qualities which he discerned in him. His methods were those which Galliéni had applied in earlier campaigns and consisted in studying the tribes, treating each one according to its individuality, counting on the support of the most influential cheikhs and advancing 'not in columns, nor by force, but like oil spilt on water, progressing step by step, playing alternately on all the local elements, utilizing the divisions and rivalries between the local tribes and between their chiefs'. M. Jonnart was convinced that, if the Quai d'Orsay, with its 'policy for windbags and eunuchs'[1] could be prevented from interfering, he could complete the

[1] Lyautey dixit.

penetration of the Oranese Sahara, pacify the border regions and eventually come to an agreement with the Sultan which would culminate in an official recognition of French influence in Morocco.

This unorthodox soldier seemed made to appreciate Isabelle, as the formalistic officers of the Arab Bureaux seemed made to misunderstand her. He had been predisposed in her favour by Victor Barrucand, who had offered, from the outset, his whole-hearted support for his policy and who was soon to become a personal friend as well as a political ally. Barrucand's enthusiasm for Isabelle had aroused his curiosity and, now that the acquaintance was made, he found her even more interesting than he had anticipated.

'She was that which attracts me more than anything else,' he wrote to Barrucand after her death. 'A rebel. What a joy to find someone who is truly himself, refusing all prejudice, all servitude, all banality, and who passes through life as freely as a bird through the air. I loved her for what she was and for what she was not. I loved that prodigious artistic temperament and everything about her that maddened the lawyers, the corporals, the mandarins of all sorts. Poor Mahmoud!'

So the great soldier, the monarchist and the aristocrat, and the poor nomad who had been hunted from El Oued and from Tenes and insulted in every gutter-newspaper in Algeria, became friends. Lyautey was an artist in his way, but also a practical man. He enjoyed Isabelle's picturesque conversation and unconventional company, but he saw immediately how he could make use of her. The success of his policy of peaceful advance into this dangerous part of the desert depended on his relations with the local tribes, with the Bedouin proprietors of the chain of oases that ran southward from Ain-Sefra down to the Desert of Stones. Many of them also owned property across the border in Morocco and were thus in a favourable position for brigandage. On the other hand, the protection of France was a more solid advantage than that of the Sultan or even of the prestigious Bou-Amama. The border tribes, too, were unpredictable. In principle loyal to France, they might at any moment be swayed by a success of the terrible old warrior or of the miracle-working Rogui who plotted in the South against the Sultan and the French indiscriminately, or by any fanatic marabout who could rouse them in the name of the Prophet.

A few conversations with Isabelle in the mess or in his private office had convinced Lyautey that she was the ideal collaborator for the task he had set himself. Reports came to him of the respect with which she was received in the surrounding villages, of the admiration with which the cheikhs listened to her discourse and the confidence inspired by her possession of the Qadrya chaplet. She was in a unique position for sounding the opinion of the tribes and even for influencing them and persuading them that their interest lay in accepting French protection. For her part Isabelle, who had never ceased to protest against the repressive colonial policy of the Bureaux, believed that Lyautey's humane methods, if he were given freedom to carry them out, would bring peace and prosperity to the Moslems of Algeria and, eventually, of Morocco. Perhaps she was not averse from proving that the vague accusations of anti-French activities that had always pursued her were unfounded. After the persecution and misunderstanding to which she had become accustomed, Lyautey's friendship and confidence were immeasurably precious to her. She asked nothing better than to serve their common ideal, especially as it made it possible for her to lead the sort of life she preferred without interference. Thus she became, for a time at least, one of the most important agents of the *Deuxième Bureau* in the region, but an unofficial one treating directly with the Commander-in-Chief himself. Lyautey's intelligence service depended a good deal on such agents, but most of them were natives and passed their reports through the usual channels, while Isabelle's position remained unorthodox and undefined.

Although Lyautey had his own reasons for keeping the friendship secret, it soon became a subject for gossip in Ain-

Sefra. Isabelle spent most of her evenings in the Foreign Legion canteen, and soon became a comrade whom the legionaries accepted on equal terms. She took no trouble to hide her real identity from them and they probably knew more about her affairs than she realized, but most of them had something to hide on their own account and questions were not encouraged.

One of these legionaries, a German named Richard Kohn, wrote a revealing letter after Isabelle's death to her old friend Robert Randau, in which he described the evenings passed in her company and added some astute observations of his own:

'You can imagine how we crowded round her as soon as she arrived in the canteen. Our ignorance of the French language cut us off from the outside world and the legionaries had been on pretty bad terms with the civilians of Sidi-bel-Abbès, where we had recently been stationed. We really took a keen pleasure in talking in our own language to a person who spoke it with such elegance. It reminded us of home.

'She took an interest in our private lives, told us her brother had been in the Legion and questioned us on our reasons for joining it. Then she told us quantities of amusing stories, especially about her wanderings in the bled.

'Between ourselves, I must tell you that we were secretly flattered that she preferred the company of us soldiers to that of our officers. We knew that she was a friend of our chief, Lyautey; I had seen her one day sitting opposite him at a desk in the room in which he used to write his reports and where I had come to instal the electricity (I used to be an electrician by profession). They were whispering, leaning towards each other.

'But it is my duty to tell you that none of us ever thought of flirting with her. Sometimes ten or twelve of us would stay gossiping with her, but none of my comrades, any more than myself, would have permitted himself the slightest bad language in her presence. Moreover, she was not in the least flirtatious, nor at all pretty. Various people who knew her have spoken of her indecent conduct, but none of the legionaries she frequented at Ain Sefra would agree with them. There are even some who pretend that she was the mistress of Lyautey, either when he was a colonel or when he was given the rank of general. That is a pure calumny, for my mates and I often used to meet our chief in the evening, returning to the fort with girls from the dance-hall whom he brought home with him.'

In return for her services, Isabelle received occasional and meagre subsidies from the funds of the *Deuxième Bureau*, but the freedom of the region was her real reward. With a pass signed by Lyautey himself, she was free to follow troop operations within the limits of safety. The Army was in constant movement, in accordance with Lyautey's policy of 'ceaseless small operations, conducted without noise and without expenditure'. She followed the Spahis south to Figuig, where they had pushed in pursuit of the bandits, to the terror of the Foreign Office, for this was considered as Moroccan territory and the least false step might have disastrous consequences. The little town, built of reddish clay, lay at the centre of a vast palmery, a secret and mysterious place to which only two Europeans had, till now, ever penetrated. Then it became advisable to establish a second garrison in the region, and she rode with the troops along the route of the deep Wadi Saoura, whose reddish-coloured water never dried up and whose banks were verdant even in summer, to Beni-Ounif, lying in its dusty valley, enclosed by arid hills.

Within a few hours the sleepy little village, where a small post had existed since the previous year, had become a centre of activity. Barracks were hastily constructed; an improvised railway line stopped short, suddenly, cut off at the edge of the desert; tattooed beauties and a few camp followers from the Levant and the Northern Mediterranean came to reinforce the local brothel; groups of *goumiers* patrolled ceaselessly on their tough little Arab horses into the hills and down to the palm plantations where brigands might shelter. The outpost roasted in pitiless heat. Horses and mules hung their heads to the ground, overwhelmed by the sun; the Arabs at work on the construction of the station hardly troubled to hide their apathy and the Europeans were feverish and bad-tempered, feeling their pulses for the sign of malaria.

Lyautey was there, temporarily installed with his staff in a many-storied Arab house, surrounded, in the manner of the country, with moucharabias and tessellated balconies. He held long conversations with Isabelle, discussing with her the best means of leading the tribes to support the French penetration. Lyautey understood the subservience of this people to its religious leaders and perceived from the beginning that they could be influenced only through their marabouts. The power of the cheikhs of the various confraternities that dominated in the region—the Rahmanya, the Zianya, the Qadrya—did not stop at or recognize the frontier. To gain the ear of an important cheikh of one of these orders was to be heard among the Moroccan tribes and to contribute powerfully to the intangible conquest of which Lyautey dreamed. Isabelle, learned in Koranic science and initiated into the esoteric mysteries of the somewhat unorthodox Islam of North Africa, was a welcome guest at any *zaouia* she cared to visit and was perhaps the only European in a position to have private and informal interviews with the leading marabouts. Moreover, the budget of the Intelligence Service was severely limited at this time and it was an unusual advantage to possess a trustworthy agent who asked for no more retribution than the freedom to ride at her will from oasis to oasis and the payment of such small sums as would enable her to live in the simplest native style and give her horse better care than she would ever give herself.

So she was at liberty to follow the troops between Ain-Sefra and Figuig, between Figuig and Beni-Ounif, or to ride with a single escort to the outlying oases, to note the sounds and colours of that desolate and ardent country, crouch beside the Negro slaves and listen to their lamentable stories, visit the Beni-Israel, the Jewish tribes who lived so humbly, in filth and poverty, under the yoke of their Moslem masters.

Sometimes she served as guide to the French journalist, Jean Rodes, who had come to the Figuig to represent *Le Matin* and to an old acquaintance, the painter Maxime Noiré, from whom the Government had commissioned a panorama of the landscape, so that a thrilled French public might participate more fully in the manœuvres. Isabelle shared with them the only available room in overcrowded Beni Ounif, sleeping on a mattress in one corner and writing her articles for *Akhbar* and *La Vigie Algérienne* at the rickety table that served all three for working and eating. Both the men became greatly attached to Isabelle, after the first shock occasioned by the crudity and cynicism of her conversation had passed off and they had become accustomed to the emotional instability that made her an unpredictable and often uncomfortable companion. They looked to her for information on this strange country where even Noiré, who had spent most of his life among the Arabs, could not venture among the tribes without her protection. In return, they consoled her in the outbreaks of apparently reasonless despair that seized her from time to time, restrained her imprudence as far as they could and treated her with the same sort of ironic affection that Randau and Marival had shown for her.

Lyautey's appreciation of Isabelle did not prevent him keeping her on such short funds that it became almost impossible for her to maintain herself. It is true that her needs were so simple and she had become so accustomed to privation that such questions had little importance for her, but she had come into possession of a horse—a horse such as she had always dreamed of—a pure-bred Arab, swift and sure and fragile. For his upkeep she must have money. He must have oats, he must be kept clean, silk-coated and in fine condition. On his behalf she was ready to beg for the funds she would never have asked for herself. Lyautey, perhaps through caprice or perhaps through motives of his own, refused for weeks at a time to receive her in his office. Perhaps he found it convenient, in the interest of his service, to appear to disown a relationship which would have diminished her usefulness as an agent if it had become public property. At any rate there were times when she was reduced to writing pitiful little notes, begging to be received, to be accorded a tiny subsidy from the funds of the *Deuxième Bureau* with which to buy fodder.[1] Lyautey replied or not, according to his humour of the moment, and Isabelle lived in uncertainty, never sure of her reward, bringing precious information that often indicated the points at which it would be possible to advance without danger or where a certain tribe remained hostile and must be brought to better sentiments before its territory could be entered without combat.

At the same time she was ceaselessly noting her impressions of this savage country, seeking the phrase that would portray the outline of a half-ruined village profiled against a leaden sky; the image of a pair of Berber women, draped in their heavy purple robes, passing along a sun-drenched road; the peace of a night of Ramadan, at Géryville, and the Bedouin soldiers improvising their love songs that resembled a long cry of pain.

Isabelle had indeed attained some of her ambitions. She had the freedom she had always longed for, the appreciation of her entourage and a small measure of recognition in the Press. But these things had come too late. Life had been too hard for her and she had passed through too many privations. Her health had resisted longer than any normal woman's could have done, but it had finally succumbed, and she was now a mere wreck, suffering from such multiple diseases that they could hardly be distinguished one from the other. The only life that she could bear to lead was a life that must inevitably kill her. It was written, just as it was written that she was never to live in peace with the weak, gentle man she still loved nor know any joys except the transient ecstasies of the vagabond.

[1] This correspondence between Isabelle and Lyautey has been destroyed, but a retired officer who was in charge of the *Deuxième Bureau* at Ain-Sefra in 1919 has assured me that they were, at that period, still preserved in the archives and quoted a letter in which Isabelle implored an advance of fifty francs to be devoted to the purchase of fodder.

Lyautey understood her, by instinct, and perceived under the mask of cynicism the persistent, gnawing melancholy that was the heritage of the de Moerders and was to destroy one member after another of that unlucky family.

No one, indeed, could be deceived now by the careless exterior that had for so long concealed the true Isabelle. The mask had worn thin and Lyautey was not alone to guess the truth. One of his officers, who knew her well at this time, wrote after her death:

'Although she never complained, she revealed a bitter disappointment. She was a woman who expected nothing more from life. Although she was not yet thirty years old, all seduction had disappeared in her. She was ravaged by drink. Her voice had become harsh, she had lost all her teeth and shaved her head like a Moslem. Sometimes she used to visit us at the mess (at Ain-Sefra). One evening I was there with her and some comrades when someone knocked at the window, his tall figure profiled against the glass. It was Lyautey making his evening rounds.

'With that frank manner of an elder brother that he used to us, he cried joyfully:

' "There's a good time going on here. May I come in?"

'The evening ended gaily. Lyautey had a great admiration for Isabelle Eberhardt and her intelligence. He used to say: "No one understands Africa as she does." '

★   ★   ★

By the end of November, winter had fallen on the High Plateaux and the dunes were white with a snow that would lie, at that altitude, for the next three months. Isabelle suffered from the cold and the grey desolation of this desert land where 'the only luxury is the sun' and which appears morose and forbidding under a clouded sky. Lyautey had ridden southwards to defy Bou-Amama and establish a post in the region of Bechar, in Moroccan territory.[1] Victor Barrucand wrote that

[1] Lyautey baptised the post Colomb, after the General of that name. When the Foreign Office, terrified at this intrusion into the Sultan's lands,

she was needed in Algiers; Sliman, deserted for over three months, begged for an interview with his elusive wife. In December, Isabelle set off for the North, accompanied by a native soldier, and a huge, black, hairy dog that had been her companion during the solitary expeditions of the summer.

From Ain-Sefra she rode to Géryville, nearly three thousand feet up in the Plateaux, then on again through the Jebel Amour and the mountains of the Ouled Naïl, with their ragged peaks, chasms and resounding waterfalls. In all this desolate land there was no shelter to be found, save in a few widely dispersed posts and occasionally under the tent of some nomad bound for the more hospitable South. The journey had to be accomplished on mules, since the climate was too hard for horses or camels.

At the halts, after the exhausting day, it was delicious to creep into the close warmth; to hold out frozen hands to a crackling wood fire and drink the boiling coffee or mint tea that was brought on great brass trays to the starving travellers. When Isabelle was warmed and refreshed, she would sit for a little while, listening to the talk of the servants or of the occasional soldiers who took refuge in these mountain shelters, or of Bedouin hosts who told in the Berber dialect long stories of forgotten heroes or discussed the prospects of pasturage in distant oases.

It was thus that she inscribed one day the melancholy song of a young Spahi, Mohammed ould Abd-el-Kader, who had claimed like herself the hospitality of a Bedouin tent near Aflou, high in the Jebel Amour. They lay stretched in the steamy warmth, while the wind howled among the peaks, and Mohammed sang the Song of the Corpse-washer:

---

telegraphed to ask whether he realized that Bechar lay in Morocco, Monsieur Jonnart wired back that there was no question of Bechar but that troops had been moved to Colomb. As no one in Paris had heard of such a place, the Government was satisfied. Soon after, the town became known as Colomb-Bechar.

I welcome you, O pure-hearted brother!
O last visitor: you enter my tent . . .
To you and to you alone will I tell the whole truth.

I have passed through the door by which all men must pass;
Shepherds and aghas, caïds and beggars.
I will not lie to you on the threshold;
In the house of the other world
All cunning is left behind.

I believed in the friendship of blood brothers,
In the love of children born of the same flesh;
I longed for wealth under a wide tent;
I desired abundant feasts and splendid robes.

I sought the swiftness and ardour of stallions,
And the strength of arm that is man's honour,
And modesty that crowns the brow of a woman.

But the hour is come
And the angel of death has approached me;
I have lain down and I welcome you,
O washer of corpses: last friend left to me!

From you my body will have a last caress;
Through you I shall come by the shroud
That will be my white robe of eternity.

When I shall be safe in the tomb's refuge,
When the hearts of the Moslems
Shall have prayed the last prayer for me,
I shall soon be forgotten, my name will be forgotten,
For my name was given for life.

O washer of corpses, when two years shall have passed
Ask the thorns that grow on my tomb
What tears my friends shed on them,
What lamentations enchant the wind.

They will tell you: The rain from the sky
And the song of the birds that must die in their turn,
The rain from the sky and the song of the birds
To the Glory of Him who will never die.

But such comforting moments were few, and the hardships of the journey exhausted Isabelle more than any journey she had ever undertaken. The roads were often blocked by snow, and it was not till she reached Berrouaghia, far in the North, that she was able to join the railway line that would bring her to Algiers.

Barrucand awaited her, enthusiastic for her adventures, but reproachful for her laziness, for only a few rare articles had reached him. However, she had brought with her a manuscript entitled 'Southern Oran', which began to appear in *Akhbar* at the New Year and which continued, as a serial, until June 1904. Other articles appeared in *La Dépêche Algérienne* and *La Vigie Algérienne*, and for the first time her astonishing faculty of 'seeing' the essential poetry of Africa began to be recognized. But Algiers[1] was for her the North, the corrupt town which she despised, and suffered in despising, since she desired only to understand and sympathize with all the world.

'We are all poor devils,' she said to Barrucand one day, 'and those who refuse to understand that are even poorer than ourselves.'

[1] An aged colonist who remembers encountering her in the streets of Algiers during this visit, described to me succinctly the impression she made on him: 'A scrofulous little Arab . . . certainly tubercular'.

Chapter Sixteen

WHEN Isabelle returned to Ain-Sefra in May 1904, she found the situation in the district greatly changed for the better. Everywhere there were signs of the success of Lyautey's policy. At the Friday market, merchants arrived in safety from the neighbouring villages, without fear of the marauding *djiouch*, the nomad Beni-Amour came down from the mountains with their flocks of sheep, to mingle, superb and disdainful, with the sedentary tribes of the Figuig. Even the Beni-Guil, the right arm of Bou-Amama and the terror of Southern Oran, came from Morocco to buy and sell—mistrustful, half-wild people, who had taken the first step on the way to civilization, whose misery and destitution were already a little less complete. Bou-Amama himself, discouraged by the French successes, had moved farther south and was temporarily inactive.

Lyautey was absent. A month earlier he had descended on Bechar, in spite of the anxiety of the French Foreign Office, to consolidate and expand his position in the region. The first little outpost at Colomb was becoming a great military centre. From there Lyautey was sending reconnaissance units into the heart of Moroccan territory, among the once implacable Beni-Guil, and meeting with no opposition. The situation was full of possibilities that could hardly have been dreamed of a couple of years earlier. Lyautey's letters to his sister, to the Viscount de Voguë, to his old chief, Galliéni, were full of his plans for the barbaric neighbour-country: 'We must digest Morocco, not conquer it', he wrote to his sister, and the slow process of digestion was already beginning. In fact, Lyautey was encountering less hostility in Morocco than from certain elements among the Arab Bureaux, whose jealousy and mistrust so often hampered his advance.

Isabelle soon made herself familiar with the situation, which she had already heard copiously discussed in Algiers. She burned to join the troops at Colomb-Bechar, but could not get permission to go further south than Beni-Ounif. It was there that she visited Lyautey on his return and that he proposed to her the astonishing expedition that was to be the culmination of her career as a Moslem, as an artist and as his collaborator.

On November 14th of the preceding year, Lyautey had written a long account of the Algero-Moroccan situation to the old General Galliéni whom he still considered as his master and to whom he regularly confided his hopes, his plans and his disappointments.

'It seems to me', he wrote, 'that the aid of the marabout of Kenadsa—with whom it is essential to get in touch again and who must be persuaded to return as quickly as possible from Tafilalet—would be one of the most important factors in our success.'

Kenadsa lay to the south-west of Colomb-Bechar, beyond the frontier region, and acknowledged the suzerainty of the Sultan of Fez. The only real authority, however, came from the *zaouia*, the mother-house of the Confraternity of the Zianya, founded there in the eighteenth century by El Hadj M'Hammed-ben-bou-Zian, who claimed to be the 'continuator' of the holy teacher and reformer, Sidi Chadeli.

Kenadsa was, in fact, a tiny theocratic state, in which the marabout ruled, administered justice, settled disputes and held almost absolute dominion. The *khouans* of the Zianya submitted to him not only in spiritual but in temporal matters. They were wild Berbers, untamed and hostile to any foreign influence, and a word from their marabout would have sent them campaigning joyfully with Bou-Amama's *djiouch* or the Rogui's ferocious bands. It was only the fact that their cheikhs had shown themselves in general favourable to the French which had held them in check.

The present marabout of Kenadsa, Sidi Brahim ould Mohammed was—as Lyautey's letter indicated—hesitating before throwing the weight of his influence on the French side. It was essential to gain his support before commencing the penetration of the region, for Si Brahim, in addition to the traditional authority of his position, had a widespread personal prestige which made his word law within an area extending far beyond the immediate environment of the village. He was respected by learned Moslems throughout Algeria and Morocco and students from all North Africa crowded to the *zaouia* to hear his teaching. He was considered as an austere, holy man and the *zaouia* had the reputation of being one of the few centres in which the Sufi doctrine was practised in its strict integrity.

The first step in the peaceful conquest of Kenadsa had already been taken—Si Brahim had been persuaded to return to his *zaouia*. The second must be to convince him that his interests and those of his people could best be served by collaborating with the French. Isabelle, initiated into a friendly confraternity and accustomed to frequent the *zaouia* and the marabouts of many sects, seemed to Lyautey the ideal agent to undertake this delicate work of persuasion.

Isabelle's acceptance was joyful and immediate. Everything about the scheme appealed to her. She who had longed to visit Colomb-Bechar, could now penetrate yet farther into the forbidden area, into the mysterious regions that had remained hidden for so long from all Europeans. She would have the unique opportunity of living the life of a Koranic student over a long period instead of merely being received as a visitor. Strange reports, often scandalous, circulated about the customs of these students; no one had ever published the exact truth about their lives. Avid for every detail she could learn of Moslem life, enamoured of mystery and attracted by all that was colourful and romantic, she felt that the journey would finally enable her to penetrate to the heart of Islam. She probably even took her mission seriously, for Isabelle was easily influenced, her enthusiasm quickly aroused, and the conversation of Lyautey had opened up to her imagination wonderful perspectives of an ideal Moslem state prospering under the enlightened tutorship of France and directed by a humane policy imposed by the great General.

The way to Colomb-Bechar led through Bel-Houari and the Desert of Stones. The heat was so intense that Isabelle, noting the impressions of the day at each night's halt, wrote that a reddish vapour seemed to dance on the horizon and that blood trickled constantly from the parched nostrils of her horse. Her escort was a good-humoured *mokhazni*, inventive, handy at cooking meals of fragrant potatoes in hollows scooped in the sand. There were halts at villages where dour Spaniards and homesick Legionaries welcomed the 'little Spahi', plied her with harsh red wine and told endless tales of the desert till the night wore away and it was time to start again.

These were the fever regions, plagued by the malaria-bearing mosquitoes that bred in the *chotts*; then, farther on, came the 'country of thirst', the desert of pale sand, well-less, that reminded her, for the first time in Southern Oran, of the white dunes of El Oued. Water was scarce, almost unobtainable, and the mirage shone and faded constantly on the horizon—elusive, cool lakes that dissolved into puffs of blue smoke at the traveller's approach. Here, in this untouched region, on the route to the Unknown, she could taste the only joy that did not bring its inevitable disappointment. She imagined herself as the eternal Vagabond, to whom destitution and joy were synonymous.

'Near the dying fire lay the vagabond, rolled in his burnous.

'With his head resting on his bent arm, his limbs weary, he gave himself up to the infinite pleasure of sleeping alone, sleeping on the kindly earth, in a nameless corner of the desert where he would never pass again.'

After this liberty in the great, anonymous spaces of the desert, Colomb and Bechar seemed to Isabelle sad and enervating with their dark, roofed lanes, their crumbling hovels and the ugly, unfinished buildings of the garrison adding to the impression of discomfort and disorder. She despised the sedentary ksar-dwellers, comparing them to the fierce, free Bedouin and the hardy mountain tribes. She was impatient to leave these busy military centres for the mysterious domain of Sidi Brahim, where she alone had the right to penetrate.

At last the preparations were complete. The chief of the *khouans* of Bechar gave her a Negro slave, named Embarek, for guide; she carried a letter of introduction from a leading *khouan* of Ain-Sefra. Her safety and welcome were assured.

After a long ride, broken by halts, she arrived within sight of Kenadsa—'a large ksar built of dark, warm coloured clay, behind fine gardens of a splendid green. The ksar clings to the gentle slope of a small hill, in the graceful disorder of superimposed terraces. To the right, the golden dune, with its table-topped stone formation, rises almost steeply. A white *qoubba* shelters the tomb of a Moslem woman of the family of the founder of Kenadsa and the Confraternity of the Zianya —Lella Aicha. Around the *qoubba* are innumerable graves which are gradually disappearing beneath the sand; they seem like a border country before arriving at the dwellings of the living. All the cities of the Sahara are preceded by cemeteries.'

Embarek guided her through the maze of narrow lanes to the *zaouia*, where they were received by several slaves, to whom he introduced her by the name under which he knew her himself—Si Mahmoud ould Ali, a young Tunisian student travelling from *zaouia* to *zaouia* for his instruction. After a long wait, a tall Negro slave came to her, respectfully kissed the cords of her turban and led her across a great courtyard and through a low door pierced in a massive, windowless wall, into a large, square room.

A dim light filtered through an opening in a ceiling composed of wooden beams, arranged in pattern and supported by four pillars built into the walls. A narrow staircase of blackened stone led up to a terrace on the roof and in a recess in the wall stood a small iron stove, the smoke of which could escape through a hole pierced in the ceiling. In the centre of the room was a small pond, hollowed in the floor, with a jug of water standing beside it for washing purposes. The clay walls and the ceiling were greenish black and shining with age. The wooden door was painted with faded flowers.

The strangeness of the décor, the silence of the place and some incertitude as to her welcome, made Isabelle uneasy. The slaves had brought her the symbols of hospitality—carpets, tea and fresh water—but she was now, and for the first time, outside the French zone. The adventure at Behima had marked her. Here she could look to no one for protection. Yet the hermit in her rejoiced at the perspective of long months of meditation in this quiet and sanctified abode, far from all interference from the outside world and far from the petty persecutions of narrow-minded Europeans that had darkened her whole life in Africa.

The entry of Si Brahim finally reassured her, for there was nothing wild or savage in his appearance. He was a tall, stout man, with a face pitted by smallpox and a fringe of greying beard. His gestures were slow and dignified, his smile gentle and welcoming. He wore simple, white garments under a *haik* of thin wool. His head-dress was a large turban, wound round a *chechya*, without the veil framing the face that was part of the Algerian head-dress. His type seemed to her partly that of the Moroccan townsmen—for he spoke with their lisping accent—and partly that of the villagers of the South.

Isabelle, accustomed to the free and easy atmosphere of the Algerian *zaouias*, never completely understood Si Brahim's spiritual rôle as marabout of Kenadsa. She saw for herself that the maraboutic influence made of the town a sort of haven of peace, where poverty was unknown—since any destitute person could claim the hospitality of the *zaouia*; where there were few disputes—since these were commonly brought before the marabout for settlement. She saw that in matters of policy, his word was law, that it was he who dispensed justice, whose authority was that of a feudal lord or petty king rather than the chief of a relatively small religious community.

But Si Brahim's position was even more mysterious and complicated than it appeared on the surface. He was a Moroccan, and in Morocco Islam was more exigent and austere than among the Algerian tribes. Kenadsa was a Sufi retreat in the strict sense of the term. Silence, isolation and fasting were imposed on the inmates and they might undertake nothing without the consent of their cheikh, whose essential function was to teach the love of the Unique Being to his *khouans*.

No less than twenty qualifications, applicable in all the different confraternities, and designed to augment his spiritual authority, were required of a cheikh, and if, in the majority of Algerian *zaouias*, the rigour of the rules had been relaxed, they retained all their force in the mother-house of the Zianya. Si Brahim's rôle was to lead his novices along all the degrees of the Mystic Path—beginning with the simple observance of the external forms of the law, continuing along the Path of Truth and arriving by gradual stages at that point where the faithful disciple, favoured at last with the gift of ecstasy, is able to tear aside, for a moment at least, the veil that shrouds Absolute Truth.

The austere rule by which Sidi Brahim strove to assure the purification of his students did not at first trouble Isabelle's contentment. She was content to meditate, to write and occasaionally to gossip with the Negro slaves. Gradually, however, the inaction began to weigh on her; it began to dawn on her that she was less of a guest than a prisoner. The doors were barred, and when she attempted to wander past the courtyard, there was always a silent slave standing in her passage. Soon she understood a thing which was never implicitly expressed —she might not leave the *zaouia* without the permission of the marabout. She was astonished and uneasy. She had never been used to restraint, and seems to have been ignorant of the general rule by which no novice might leave the building in which he studied, except with the leave of his cheikh, who would question him on his reason for wishing to absent himself, where he was going and for how long he desired to remain away. She had never dreamed of submitting herself to such discipline, and after a week of seclusion, she sent a slave to beg Si Brahim for an interview.

Si Brahim was perfectly aware of Isabelle's real identity, although he affected, in the courteous Arab fashion, to believe in the reality of Si Mahmoud. He was not astonished to hear that this European, whose Moslem affinities were not entirely clear, had come to the *zaouia* without understanding the régime that was followed by all who took shelter within its walls. He was a tolerant, kindly man and he had good reasons for showing indulgence to the protégée of Lyautey. So he made no difficulties and gave Isabelle permission to come and go at her will, only warning her to exchange her Algerian costume for the light *djeleba* and thin muslin turban of the Moroccans. The Algerians in this fanatic country were despised as renegades who had sold themselves to the French, and her appearance in the town, clothed in burnous, *haik* and swathed turban, might have aroused a hostile demonstration.

Isabelle was free now to wander at her will and to mingle for the first time with the natives of a country fiercer and more intransigent than Algeria, proud of an ancient civilization which had never existed in its neighbour country, jealous of ancient traditions. She was able to assist at the strange festivals of the Soudanese slaves—who were in fact, slaves only in the *zaouia*, but who possessed their own homes and property and lived as free men outside its precincts. They were Moslems on the surface, but remained at heart the fetish-worshippers that their fathers had been when they were first brought in captivity to the West and their ceremonies recalled the ancient days of Voodoo, the sacrifices and unbridled ritual dances of their ancestors.

She came to know the crowded Mellah, which seemed to her, in spite of all its filth and poverty, like an immense magic-lantern, with its marvellous Jewesses—impure for the Arabs, so that, for all their sensual and immodest beauty, they remained as if invisible for the men of the other race; the swarming children and the humble men, accustomed by centuries of scorn and oppression to protect themselves by meekness and ruse. Then she could wander on the dunes, dotted with the little *qoubbas* where slept the saints of the Zianya and where the nomad women of the Douo-Menia, lean and magnificent Gypsies, naked beneath their rags, strode like empresses, unabashed before the men of the village. High on the dune there lived a crazy 'marabout', whose madness alone had earned his reputation for sanctity. To his retreat came all the *kif* addicts of the district, to stupefy themselves and attain, to the chorus of his prophecies, a beatitude of their own. Isabelle soon found her way there and was able to spend long hours, stretched on the filthy floor, noticing neither dirt nor vermin nor evil smells, lost in the trance of the drug.

Yet the life in the *zaouia* itself was so active and so varied, now that she was free to wander about it at her will, that she found in it an endless source of study and observation. In the evening, after the last prayer, she would retire to the silent room which had appeared so menacing at first and write, in the thick note-books that comprised the greater part of her baggage, all that had happened during the day: the comings and goings of nomad chieftains, of sellers of sheep, of those who brought their grievances to the cheikh and those who brought letters telling of the razzias of Bou-Amama and the pillaging of the Rogui. The *zaouia* was the centre of constant movement, yet nothing could disturb the essential calm of the place or spoil a peace so profound that days and nights seemed to pass in a long dream.

It was this stillness and peace that Isabelle most loved in Kenadsa and that she evoked most often in the manuscript that was destined to be published, in such dramatic circumstances, under the title of *Dans l'ombre chaude de l'Islam*.

' In the gardens', she wrote, 'the last hour of the heat passes for me in quiet contemplation, in lazy conversations broken by long silences.

' At the *moghrab*, when the sun has gone down, we go to pray in the *hamada* which lies just in front of the great cemeteries and the *qoubba* of the blessed Lella Aicha, where the whiteness is gradually taking on an iridescent quality.

'Everything is calm, dream-like and smiling, at this charming hour.

'Women pass, bare-footed, in the direction of the well of Sidi-Embarek. The men, who have been gossiping, half-lying on the ground, rise up with the astonishingly noble movement that seems like a daily-renewed resurrection.

'A great murmur of prayer rises up from this corner of the desert.

'When the prayer is finished, groups of men remain crouched on the spread burnouses; their fingers tell over the red chaplets, black chaplets . . . from their lips, in a half-whispered chant, rise the litanies of the Prophet.

'. . . To possess a healthy body, purified of all stain after bathing in cool water, to be simple and to believe, never to have known doubt, never to have struggled against oneself, to await without fear or impatience the inevitable hour of eternity—therein lies the peace and joy of Islam, and—who knows?—perhaps wisdom also lies therein.'

Now she was spending much of her time in the company of Sidi Brahim, who often invited her to his apartments to meet visitors from different regions of North Africa, or to assist him as secretary in difficult negotiations with the rapacious Bedouin. The marabout must have had conversation with her on spiritual subjects too. Perhaps he initiated her into his confraternity—since her membership of the Qadrya would not exclude adherence to certain other sects. But Isabelle maintained an almost inexplicable discretion on such matters. She had never recorded the substance of the important conversation she had had with Lella Zeyneb at El Hamel, and now, although she frequently quoted in her diary Si Brahim's opinions on local matters and even the political situation, she made never a mention of his religious teaching. She was writing with the idea in her mind that one day her notes would be read and published, and probably felt herself bound to protect the esoteric doctrine that was transmitted to her by saintly men and women who had advanced so far on the Path of Truth. So she was silent on the subject that most preoccupied her—a worthy vessel for secret teachings.

★   ★   ★

Often, as she wandered in the labyrinthine *zaouia* or attended prayer at the mosque, Isabelle came on the pale and silent young students attached to the establishment. She knew nothing of how or where they lived, what were their private lives or from whence they came. Their corporate existence was hidden from all strangers. In fact, the life of these Moroccan *talebs* was so mysterious that it had given rise to disquieting stories[1], and even Isabelle felt some hesitation before accepting an invitation, brought to her by one of the slaves with precautions that did nothing to reassure her, to take tea with them in their apartments. In spite of misgivings, she accepted.

'We enter the reception-room by a double door, sculptured and groaning on its rusty hinges. It is filled with a vaporous half-light, its aspect rendered agreeable by several

---

[1] A few years earlier, the French explorer Auguste Moulièras, had published a sensational book entitled *Le Maroc inconnu*, in which he described at length the life of the Moroccan *zaouias* and that of the students attached to them. M. Moulièras' method was to begin his recital with some phrase such as: 'I would that my right hand might be cut off rather than be obliged to transcribe the horrors which I nevertheless feel it my duty to recount' . . . and then to describe with unconcealed relish the orgies which were alleged to take place in these circles. Isabelle had read the book, and this accounts for the—momentary—hesitation she felt in accepting the invitation of the *taleb*, Si-Madani. Since then it has transpired that M. Moulièras had never set foot in Morocco and was writing from hearsay.

delicate pillars, their milky stone carved with a lacework of arabesques. Small windows cut out of a dome in the ceiling open on to the watered silk of the sky, throwing a pale light on the Nile-green tiles that decorate the wall to the height of my head and line the worn floor.

'A stone step leads up to the other half of the vast room, which is slightly raised, the floor carpeted with rugs from Rabat and mattresses of white wool.

'Beneath the black beams, interwoven with rushes dyed in red and black that form the ceiling, an inscription in vermilion lettering runs round the whole length of the walls: El afia el bakia—"eternal health".

'In little niches, on shelves, piled on coffers decorated with flowers of faded gold, are amassed all kinds of objects: Arabic books, kitchen utensils, clothes and saddlery; musical instruments and weapons, all mixed together in a charming confusion. In contrast to the vulgar pottery brought from Bechar, a graceful jug of Venetian glass stands out by the rare shades of its crystal.

'Here are long-beaked copper lamps, a green pot adorned with clover pattern, tiles stained with melted colours and, to complete the pleasure of the eye, the many-coloured little glasses are like wild flowers spread on the fine tea-tray, beneath a length of brilliant silk. . . .

'Faridji, the slave, and his brother Khaddou, set fire to dried palms in the courtyard, while Si-Madani explains, although I have put no question to him, the reason for the mysterious way in which the Negro brought me the invitation.

' "You know, Si Mahmoud, that custom and convention require that our parents and elders should know nothing of our pleasures, or should at least pretend to know nothing of them. We meet here to pass the time in delighting our hearts with music or the recitation of the sublime works of the ancient poets, or in cordial conversation. No one, except God and ourselves, must know what goes on here. . . . If it were otherwise, and in spite of the innocence of our pleasures, we should feel deeply ashamed of them and might incur severe blame. That is why I have chosen this apartment, the only habitable place in the old Casbah, that was left to me by my grandfather, Sidi Bou Medina. No one passes by here, there is no one to give us advice or to preside over the free delights of our minds."

'The time passes in conversation. As if to insist on the intimacy of the reunion, one of the Moslem scholars returns to his sewing after the introductions have been made, and busies himself choosing silks for the white *gandourah* which he is decorating with delicate embroidery. Sewing and embroidery are popular with the Moroccan students and are considered as a proof of good taste. There is no dishonour in doing this work in public.

'El-Madani takes a three-stringed guitar and begins to sing carelessly, humming a languid old Andalusian song, the motif of which turns constantly around the same note. His cousin, Mouley Idris, a puny adolescent with a yellowish complexion, accompanies him softly on a tambourine. The handsome Hamiani Abd-el-Djebbar yawns at the music; he remains stretched out at full length on the carpet, like a great deerhound, stretching his muscles, exasperated by inaction.

'I listen to the sad, languorous song, and I reflect on the lives of these Moslem students.

'They will study for years within the austere compass of ancient mosques. There will be pious exercises which most of these young men, affiliated as they are to one or other of the mystical confraternities, carry to the length of attaining each day to a state of ecstasy. Under all this imposed austerity, there hides a simple gaiety, an ardent sensuality which leads to the most complicated adventures and, it must be admitted—and especially here in the West—to many hidden vices. . . . The exteriorization of pleasure, so dear to European students, is unknown in Islam. The scholars of Morocco are trained from early youth to conceal their joys. Thus is explained their ardent but reserved nature, their violent interior passions which show so little on the surface, their voluptuous intellectuality which fades so soon.'

And thus the blazing months of summer passed by and the life of the *zaouia* became so familiar to Isabelle that she hardly realized its strangeness any more. To penetrate so profoundly into an existence as yet almost unsuspected by any European, soon seemed so natural that it was the old, agitated life of Algiers and Ain-Sefra that began to appear unreal. In the deep quietness of her room, enclosed by walls green with age and bathed in constant twilight, the journalist and the adventuress began to fade before the mystic. Now, for the first time since the happy days of El Oued, she had leisure to reflect on the great problems of life; on the relationship between man and God, and the difficult inter-relation of holiness, love and sensuality that had never ceased to torment her.

'The heart should never be given to any human, because it belongs only to God; to take delight in all human beings is a means of doing homage to their Creator; one must never seek oneself in another, but in oneself alone.

'I bless my solitude which allows me to *believe*, which is making of me once more a simple and exceptional creature, resigned to my destiny.'

Her destiny was indeed approaching—that ultimate destiny, the encounter between man and God, which, for Isabelle, was the culminating point of all existence, the ultimate and heroic moment of Truth.

*   *   *

The climate of Kenadsa was unhealthy and malaria was rife in the district. Isabelle had been subject for years to increasingly violent attacks of the disease and conditions in her damp and murky apartment in the ancient *zaouia* made it inevitable that she should be almost constantly ill. When the fever was on her, she would lie for hours, and often days at a time, in a sort of trance, watching the procession of visions that passed before her eyes. When she emerged from her delirium, she would find herself stretched out on the terrace, where she had been carried by the servants, or else in her own room, where a tall Sudanese slave, squatting beside her mattress, fanned her slowly with a great palm leaf. Tea and food, which she had not the strength to eat, were brought to her regularly from the mother of Si Brahim, who watched over her, invisibly but with unfailing attention.

Often, as she listened to the courteous messages brought to her from 'Lella' by the slave, or toyed with the dishes sent from her to the invalid, Isabelle speculated on the life of this strange woman, whose authority was felt everywhere but who was never seen. Isabelle would never know whether she resembled her son, whether she had the gentle manners of Lella Zeyneb or the proud bearing of the women of the Souff. All the Arab women must remain for her mysterious and apart. It was inherent in her equivocal position that she might have no dealing with them. Here she must never abandon the rôle of Si Mahmoud, for whom it would be a sin to regard the face of a woman.

On the days when she had sufficient strength, Isabelle would drag herself out to the charming little garden where Si Brahim received his visitors. She rested there, tried to write, but as the terrible heat of August beat down on the town, her strength began to fail entirely and she felt that her courage was almost spent:

'Once more the *muezzin* cried out his melancholy call. I was quite awake now. My bruised and heavy eyelids opened avidly on the splendour of the evening. Suddenly an infinite sadness descended on me; I was filled with childish regrets.

'I was alone, alone in this lost corner of Morocco, and wherever I had lived I had been alone and should remain so wherever I went, for ever. . . . I had neither country, nor home, nor family. . . . Perhaps I had not even any friends left. I had passed through life like a stranger, arousing nothing but reprobation and aversion.

'At this moment I was suffering, far from all help, among men who would witness impassively the ruin of everything around them, who cross their arms in the face of illness and death, and say: "Mektoub!"

'Those who, in distant parts of the world, might have been thinking of me, were thinking no doubt of their own happiness. They did not suffer from my suffering. . . . Yes, really it is written.'

It was perhaps the first cry of revolt against her destiny that had ever been forced from Isabelle, but she soon surmounted her moment of weakness. As the capricious fever withdrew for a while, she regained courage. There was much to interest her, to occupy her mind. Si Brahim had asked her permission to lodge two other visitors in her room. They were a young Berber of the Ait-Atta tribe, named El-Hassani, a 'man of powder', who 'spoke with his gun'; and his Negro companion, Mouley Sahel. The two had come as emissaries of their own cheikh of the Zianya, who had commanded them to restore to his colleague at Kenadsa a certain flock of sheep, stolen from the *zaouia* some time earlier and driven off to the West. The two had taken part in the *razzia* and now returned, penitent, to ask the pardon of Si Brahim. The good old cheikh received them kindly and assured Isabelle that she would find them interesting company.

As Si Brahim had foreseen, the two young men became her friends during the short time of their stay and pressed Isabelle to return with them to the West. They would march for a whole month, passing by Guir, by Tafilalet, perhaps by Tisint. The marabout pressed her to accept their invitation, having perhaps good reasons for wishing her to visit Morocco under the guidance of his own men and to bring Lyautey reports that would be subtly flavoured with his own views. He guaranteed her safety himself:

'When one of the Ait-Atta says to you—"You are under God's finger and mine. I answer for you", you may go with him wherever he will take you. You will return safely unless both of you die together,' he told her.

But the constant fever had shaken Isabelle's confidence in herself. She feared the rigours of the journey. Although she had never cared for her health, the attack of fever had been so terrible that she realized at last that she must return to Ain-Sefra for treatment.

'Every man', the Prophet Ali is supposed to have said on the night of his assassination, 'goes out to meet the fate that awaits him; his efforts to avoid it must all be in vain; life consumes itself in the search for that secret to which God alone holds the key.' So Isabelle, in the interests of her health, renounced Tafilalet, at the foot of the Great Atlas, where the Sahara ended, and the little-known oases of the Tiout. She left Kenadsa on the same day as El-Hassani and Mouley Sahel, and they rode for a while together, until their ways parted. Then she took leave of her two friends and turned her horse's nose reluctantly towards Bechar.

Chapter Seventeen

WHEN she arrived at last at Ain-Sefra, Isabelle was in the throes of another attack of malaria, brought on by the hardships of the long journey. She entered the military hospital at once and for some time she was obliged to submit to immobility and the unwelcome discipline imposed on the sick. There, as ever when she was not possessed by the passion for wandering, her thoughts turned to Sliman. They had never ceased to correspond, to meet whenever Isabelle's strange mode of life permitted, and now she wrote begging him to visit her. Sliman obtained leave from his employment as *khodja* in the Setif and announced his arrival.

A house, or rather, a *gourbi* was rented in the lower part of the town. It consisted of two rooms, the upper one reached by an outer staircase; a terrace; walls of crumbling *toub*, roughly plastered over. Sliman settled down there and on October 20th, in spite of the opposition of the doctor, who judged that she was not sufficiently cured, Isabelle insisted on leaving hospital.

She was home at last and, as ever when the Mektoub allowed her a moment's respite from wandering, it seemed to her that her real life lay there, with her husband, in her own home, at peace and beloved in the warm shadow of Islam.

The odorous smoke of the *kif*-pipes lent an illusion of eternity to fleeting happiness. Sliman and Isabelle passed the night in the joy of reunion. Early in the morning she roused herself to go out for a little shopping. On the way, she met and had a short conversation with a young officer of the garrison, then she hurried back to Sliman and the shelter of the crumbling little hovel.

To understand the events of that day—21st October 1904 —one must realize that the town of Ain-Sefra consisted of two parts, separated by the deep bed of the wadi. On one side lay the native quarters and on the other, dominating them by a height of two or three hundred feet, stood the Redoute, or military site, on which were built the barracks, the Company offices and the officers' houses. The wadi was spanned by a bridge, but it was ordinarily dry, and the soldiers used to cross it by the goat-tracks that formed a short cut down to the lower town. There was constant coming and going between the two quarters, and Isabelle herself was accustomed to climb by these tracks up to the Redoute when she wished to visit Lyautey or her friends of the Legion.

An eyewitness, a Legionary on orderly duty at the Company offices, has described in detail the catastrophe which occurred that morning:[1]

'Towards nine o'clock, the sergeant-major sent me to take a message to the Intendancy in town. I hurried and was back in time for breakfast. . . . I had fetched my mess-tin from the kitchen and was beginning my meal on a corner of the office table, when the quartermaster, who was standing by the open door, called out: "Kohn, come and look. . . . Quick! By God, the whole village down there is going under water! And listen to that row!"

'I joined him immediately. . . . A yellow torrent of bub-

[1] The writer is the same blunt soldier who described Isabelle's visits to the Foreign Legion canteen and her friendship with Lyautey (p. 193).

bling water was rushing through the ravine of the wadi, between the town and the camp, carrying masses of rubbish, trees, *zeribas*. Now the water was invading the quarters from which I had just returned. Between the town and the Redoute was a sort of river, full of rapids and whirlpools that widened as they swirled down, and all communication was cut off. Suddenly there was a noise of thunder and I saw the bridge collapse.

'At that time of day, there were very few soldiers in civilian Ain-Sefra; the bugles had sounded for breakfast and the legionaries were at their meal. Most of the officers lived at the Redoute and took their meals at the mess. At this moment we were all assembled in front of the camp and were watching with anguish while the town disappeared beneath the flood. We asked ourselves in what way we could help the inhabitants. One of our comrades, a soldier from Lorraine, named Beck, noticed the postman, his wife and a little child, clinging to the roof of their house, in imminent danger of death. Beck was a fine chap and tried to assist the poor wretches. He threw himself into the water, but could not overcome the current. He had just risen from his meal; he was seized by a congestion, and we saw him carried away, rolled over and over by the current, and disappear before our eyes. Meanwhile the roof on which the postman and his family had taken refuge, and where they were screaming for help, collapsed into the rushing water and the poor things were carried away in their turn. At this moment the whole of the lower part of the native town was under water.

'It was not till four in the afternoon that some of my comrades and I managed to throw a strong rope across the torrent, where other rescuers attached it firmly. When this was done we tried to cross the wadi, which was beginning to go down, by clinging to the rope. Our efforts were all in vain. The water was freezing cold and it was impossible to remain in it for long. Lyautey sent us the order to desist, since our enterprise, as he said himself, was beyond human strength. It was not till late in the night that we managed to improvise a bridge by the light of our lanterns, utilising ammunition waggons, carts and *arabas*. The water was receding rapidly and the current diminishing.'

Meanwhile, Lyautey and his officers were watching from another part of the Redoute, equally powerless to intervene in the catastrophe. Lyautey's chief concern was for Isabelle, whom he knew to have passed the night in the lower part of the town. As soon as the flood had receded and the work of rescue was in hand, he charged one of his officers, Lieutenant de Loustel, to inquire into her fate.

De Loustel discovered almost immediately that Sliman was alive. The poor man was brought to his office in a lamentable state, hardly able to give a coherent account of his escape.

'We were on the balcony of my room on the first floor', he told the officer. 'All of a sudden, we heard a grumbling sound that seemed like a procession of lorries advancing. The noise grew louder and louder. People passed by, running. They cried out: "The wadi! The wadi!" I did not understand. The weather was clear and there was neither rain nor storm. The mass of water arrived in the bed of the ravine in an instant; it rose up like a wall; it ran like a galloping horse; it was at least two metres high; it was carrying trees and furniture, bodies of animals and men.

'I saw the danger and we fled. The torrent caught us up. I do not know how I escaped. My wife was carried away.'

According to this testimony, Isabelle's body should have been found in the bed of the wadi which, now that the water had receded, was thickly littered with wreckage of every sort. Some of the corpses had been dragged for miles by the current. Day after day passed as the fruitless search spread wider and wider. Lyautey was beside himself with impatience and anxiety. At last he ordered de Loustel, in spite of Sliman's declaration, to explore the house itself.

The *gourbi* stood on a street corner and, by some strange trick of the flood, it was the only house to have been destroyed at that point. As soon as de Loustel approached, the terrible odour rising from the ruins told him what he must expect. His men began to clear away the heaps of stone, plaster and planks. Suddenly they came on the body, crushed beneath a beam, the legs doubled beneath it and the hands clasped, in a last, instinctive gesture of defence, behind the neck.

Neither Lyautey nor anyone else could ever discover the exact truth as to Isabelle's death. She had always believed that she would die young and death had come for her when she was barely twenty-seven. She had confided to her friend Randau the strange visions that sometimes beset her as she rode in the wild regions behind Tenes, of the appearance of some ancestor from the steppes of Russia warning her of an approaching fate. Credulous and superstitious as she was, such premonitions may have seemed to her like an indication of God's will. Perhaps the resignation of the Moslem—that resignation she had striven so long to attain—caused her to await passively the accomplishment of her pre-ordained destiny. . . . Or perhaps it may be, quite simply, that she saw in that great, galloping wall of water a sudden vision of deliverance. Perhaps, after rushing down the stairs with Sliman, the first moment of panic passed, she hesitated, turned back, and preferred to solve the great Mystery that had tormented her all her life.

Lyautey himself gave the orders for her funeral in the Moslem cemetery and chose her tombstone. A simple slab of basalt at her head, engraved with a verse of the Koran, and a smaller slab at her feet, served to mark her out as a person of note in this land where the dead are discreet and ask no more than a couple of pebbles to mark the place where they lie.

He took it on himself also to inform Barrucand of the circumstances of her death:

'You can imagine', he wrote, 'how much I have been moved by the loss of our poor Isabelle Eberhardt, who had my admiration and my sympathy. I must say, between ourselves, that I cannot feel regret on her account, so greatly did I fear that she was condemned to a life of disorder and incessant disappointment.'

223

Barrucand, who had known her better and longer, must have admitted in his heart the cruel truth of this judgement. In the midst of his grief, he remembered that Isabelle had told him of the manuscripts she had been preparing. There was the second part of her impressions of Southern Oran; notes on her stay in Kenadsa; the novel at which she had been working spasmodically for years. By a curious chance, she had confided, on the very morning of her death, to the officer encountered on her last walk through the town, that she had just posted a completed manuscript to Algiers and was expecting the sum of five hundred francs from her publisher. No trace of this packet could be found, and it was finally supposed that Isabelle had, as usual, confused intention and accomplishment.

A search was organized under the direction of Lyautey himself. The legionaries who had known Isabelle, listened to her stories, shown her the photographs of their families and confided to her their nostalgia for home, raked among the dried mud where the torrent had raged, alert for any scrap of paper bearing her handwriting. Sheet by sheet, the manuscripts were brought to their commander. That which was to constitute the second part of *Sud-Oranais* and the greater part of *Trimardeur* were almost intact, but the pages which dealt with Kenadsa were so soaked and stained with mud, so torn and dispersed in such disorder, that it seemed impossible that they should ever be reconstituted. There were notes, fragments of stories, in equally bad condition. Sadly, Lyautey sealed the whole lot in a box and, considering them too precious to be trusted to the post, dispatched them by a special messenger to be delivered in person to Victor Barrucand in Algiers.

Meanwhile, the news of the terrible catastrophe had shocked the whole country. Isabelle, who had been neglected or attacked by the Press all her life, suddenly became almost a national heroine. The word had gone round that she had been a protégée of the great General, it had become known that he had organized her funeral and was personally directing the search for her manuscripts. Article after article was published on her. Edmond Claris opened the series of well-intentioned stupidities with a study entitled 'The Séverine of Algeria', in which Isabelle was depicted as an amazon defending the cause of feminism. *Le Petit Journal* rendered a more effective homage by publishing her short story, 'Amara' in which she had recounted the meeting, during the crossing from Marseilles to Philippeville, with the ex-prisoner returning home to complete his vengeance. Various French writers—generally women —wrote moving epitaphs and bad poems in her honour. Even the Parisian Press discovered the story and *Figaro* wrote that:

'One of the most curious figures in Algeria was a young woman, a Russian converted to Islam, who lived the life of the Arabs, but in male attire and under the name of Mahmoud. . . . An excellent shot and marvellous horsewoman, she took part in numerous expeditions in the desert, from which she did not always return unscathed. This sort of heroine, this cosmopolitan, was a writer of distinction in the French language. In pages impregnated with contemplative nihilism, she has evoked hallucinating visions of Tunis, of Figuig. She left an unfinished novel, *Trimardeur*.'

As for Victor Barrucand, he began to build up, almost from the day of her death, a picture of an ideal Isabelle, a sort of saint of the desert, enveloped in a halo of romanticism. Day after day, *Akhbar* published leaders exalting her personality and achievements:

'Poor, great heart, thirsting for dreams and liberty', he wrote on October 30th. 'Sensibility that could suffer with every sorrow; soul soaked like a sponge in the suffering of others . . . at last her talent is recognized and justice is rendered to her generous energy. Insults, sarcasm, calumny and vile persecution have died away before her cruel fate. . . .
'She who was reproached for her too great originality has earned her pardon. Never again will she outrage anyone by the independence of her ways. She has gone, leaving her place

to those who flouted her for lack of understanding, or rather, she has gone before them, leaving them the example of her heroic life, her folly and her genius for sympathy.

'We do not know where sleeps her body tossed by the waters, but her mind remains with us, pure and full of light as an emanation of the Algerian sun.'

Trimardeur, the version of *A la Dérive* revised and completed by Barrucand, began to appear as a serial; *Akhbar* offered 'a fine photograph, printed on vellum' of its late contributor to all new subscribers and continued to consecrate its editorials to rehabilitating her memory. For a little while the evil tongues were stilled and Isabelle was glorified into a sort of symbol of romantic liberty, transformed by Barrucand's cult into a figure as unreal as that of the spy and political agitator invented by her enemies. Then the fuss died away, people remembered her above all as one who had consistently let down the prestige of the Europeans, and, if anyone troubled to mention her, it was mostly her nuisance-value that was discussed.

It was not till sixteen years later that Victor Barrucand published the volume entitled *Dans l'ombre chaude de l'Islam*, containing the notes on her life in the *zaouia* of Kenadsa, a few sketches of South Constantine and a couple of short stories with Tunis as a background. The work had an immediate and widespread success, drew attention to Isabelle's other writings and established her work indisputably among the best literature that has been inspired by Africa.

The work of compilation had been colossal, for the manuscript had been dispersed by the flood in such a way that it presented no sort of continuity and many of the pages had been reduced to mere fragments, stained, muddied and almost illegible.

'In order to reduce the fragments to some sort of order', explained Barrucand in his introduction to the book, 'we were obliged to re-edit it from beginning to end, to connect the fragments with reflections taken from the correspondence of

Isabelle Eberhardt, from her papers, her note-books and, most often, inspired by our long conversations and fraternal collaboration.'

The book concludes with a chapter, 'Notes on Isabelle Eberhardt', in which Barrucand explained the manner in which the manuscript had come into his hands and gave an account of her life which was based partly on his own desire to idealize his heroine and partly on stories of her early life culled from Isabelle herself and which did more credit to her imagination than to her veracity.

Barrucand made the mistake—or, according to some, committed the indelicacy—of joining his name to that of Isabelle as co-author of the book and giving no indication as to the passages due to his collaboration. This method of procedure gave rise to one of the most unsavoury literary quarrels in recent history, to a trial for libel, and a campaign of mud-slinging between a number of men of letters in Paris and Algiers. All the ill that can be said of Barrucand's intervention in Isabelle's literary testament has already been said; there remains the fact that *Dans l'ombre chaude de l'Islam* is an unequalled revelation of Moslem life, impressive by the exactitude of its observations, vibrant with poetry and one of the strangest human documents that a woman has given to the world.

*   *   *

In spite of Lyautey's protection, in spite of all the efforts of her friends to rehabilitate her memory, Isabelle remains unforgiven in Algeria. It is true that a street in Colomb-Bechar bears her name and that another—discreetly situated on the little-frequented outskirts of Algiers—has been christened after her. Yet neither the passage of time nor the publication of the pathetic diaries that reveal much of the motives of an indisputably inconsequent behaviour, have sufficed to disarm hostility. A generation which knows of her only by hearsay has inherited the reprobation of its elders for the poor nomad. Neither Isabelle's talent, nor her misery, nor the inexhaustible kindness and sympathy for which her memory is loved by the Arabs of the South, are allowed to weigh against her sexual excesses. Twenty years after her death, an intelligent and usually kindly Frenchwoman, living in Algiers, said to a journalist who was collecting material for a short study on the subject: 'So you mean to write an article in honour of debauch and disorder?' And nearly half a century after the day when Isabelle stifled among the waters of Ain-Sefra, a woman of the same type said to the author of this book: 'We in Algeria appreciate the writings of Isabelle Eberhardt, but we prefer not to speak of the person.'

It is a question of relative values, a matter of opinion. One may judge Isabelle as the neurotic she undoubtedly was, the victim of a disastrous heredity and a criminal upbringing. One may see in her the adventuress, eager for sensation and ready to do anything that would bring in the small sums of money necessary to continue her chosen existence. There is the artist whose sensibility responded so immediately and completely to beauty; there is the exalted mystic who longed to die in the cause of Islam. But there is also the warm human being who could pardon every offence, who thought ill of no one, who loved the humblest and most disinherited of humanity and hated only that which was false and pretentious.

Isabelle was all of these in turn. It is useless to look for a logical thread on which to hang so chaotic an existence. Those who know the truth, or part of it, accept or refuse her according to an instinctive reaction of their own nature. Lyautey loved her for her absolute refusal to subscribe to any convention; others hated her, and still hate her, for the same reason. Isabelle's life was based on a fantastic dream of liberty. At least she had the courage to live that dream to the full, accepting the misery and degradation that its realization entailed, and proudly accepting death.

About the Author

Cecily Mackworth is Welsh but has spent most of her life in France. She came to England in 1940 and wrote *I Came Out of France,* describing her experiences during the Armistice period. She remained in London during the war, lecturing to the Army, organizing discussion clubs in Wales and contributing poems and articles to *Horizon* and other literary reviews. During this period she also wrote a life of François Villon and compiled an anthology of modern French poetry with translations by English poets. Immediately after the war she returned to Paris, but soon left for a tour of Central Europe as correspondent of a French newspaper. In 1947 she went to Palestine for the MRP journal, *L'Aube,* and repeated the visit in 1948, traveling all over the Middle East and returning to write *The Mouth of the Sword.* In the spring of 1950 she went to Algeria to hunt for letters belonging to Isabelle Eberhardt, and traveled deep into the Sahara on the invitation of the government, bringing back various studies of Moslem life and peoples. She is now living in Paris.